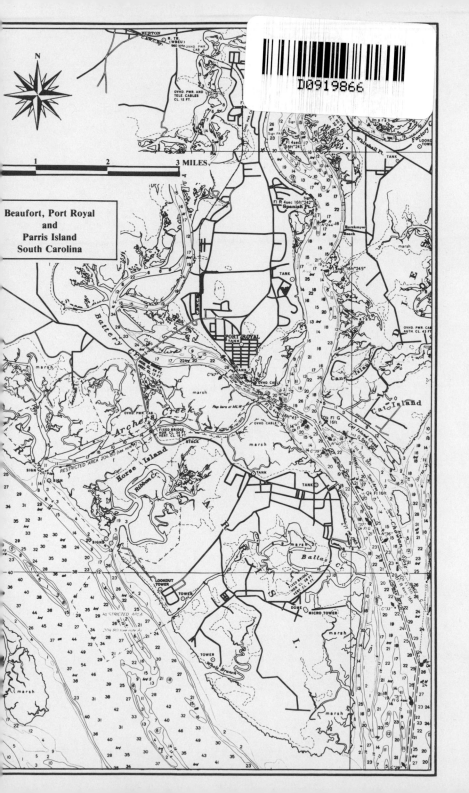

Beaufort, Port Royal
and
Parris Island
South Carolina

Rows Of Corn

Rows Of Corn

A True Account Of A Parris Island Recruit

by Herb Moore

SANDLAPPER PUBLISHING, INC.

Printed in the United States of America
Published by Sandlapper Publishing Co., Inc.
P.O. Box 1932, Orangeburg, S.C. 29116-1932

ISBN No. 0-87844-048-8

Library of Congress Cataloging in Publication Data

Moore, Herbert L., 1943-
    Rows of corn.

    1. Parris Island (S.C.: Recruit depot) 2. Moore, Herbert L.,
1943-   . 3. United States. Marine Corps--Biography. I. Title.
VE434.P3M66 1983   359.9'65'0924 [B]   83-3229
ISBN 0-87844-048-8

For those who have been there . . .
and those who question why

ACKNOWLEDGEMENTS

This book is the end result of the efforts of other people as well as my own, and I want to acknowledge their part in the endeavor.

My wife, Kathy, and two sons, Jeffrey and Gregory, put up with my late hours and lost evenings. Without their understanding and constructive criticisms, I would have bogged down before the project was completed.

To Frank Handal, who saw the need for the book and supported the project from its inception, I express my thanks.

Bill Rich, Ransom Downes, Jerry Houchins and Steve Willard not only lived the experience with me, but gave permission to use their names in their respective characters in the story.

Cathy Fletcher transformed legal pad after legal pad of my scribbled notes, inserts and additions into a readable manuscript. For her skill, dedication and patience, I shall always be grateful. Finally, there is a man named Walter Egge. You'll get to know him in this narrative but you will never know him as I do. After the manuscript was completed and in the hands of the publisher, I finally located him. I had neither seen nor spoken to him since I completed basic training, and he had no knowledge of this book until it was finished. For his leadership and courage, I am grateful. For the less obvious yet more encompassing set of values he instilled in me, I shall forever be in his debt.

CONTENTS

PREFACE

WHAT FOLLOWS IS A FACTUAL account of my experiences during the summer of 1963, specifically from June 19 until September 11. I was just out of my teens, having celebrated my twentieth birthday in January of that same year. World War II was long over, as well as the Korean War, and Vietnam was not yet a reality. John F. Kennedy was President and I had just completed my first year of college. My background was middle class, but though I had not gone in need of necessities, I certainly was not bathed in opulent wealth. I had joined the United States Marine Corps and would spend that summer going through basic training at Parris Island, South Carolina, a small island along the coast near the town of Beaufort.

The Marine Corps has been in and out of the news concerning its training tactics and techniques for decades. I am able to relate only the events surrounding one platoon's training experiences, and I will speak only for myself, not as the representative of that platoon. The names of the two junior drill instructors have been changed. The other characters depicted in this narrative are real, and I have not changed names or facts about them, to the best of my knowledge and memory.

I am not writing about innuendos or whispered accusations, but about the events I watched, felt and experienced. I share these with you, not as an exposé of the Marine Corps training techniques, but as an account by one who had to live in that system, at that place, and at that time.

I

THE ISLAND

1

P ARRIS ISLAND IS LOCATED near Beaufort, South
Carolina, almost midway between Charleston, South Carolina,
and Savannah, Georgia. It is, as its name implies, an island,
discovered by the Spanish in 1526. The first record of Marine
Corps utilization of the island was as part of a small naval station in 1891.

The Marine Corps Training Depot was established after the
turn of the century, in 1915. As a training facility for the Corps,
it reached its peak during World War II, when over two hundred
thousand recruits passed through the gates. Just under fifty
thousand were trained during the first World War, and another
one hundred thirty-eight thousand trained during the Korean
War. Estimated figures from the Marine Corps claim about fifty thousand men a year pass through the recruit training program.

The first bridge connecting the island to the mainland was
constructed in 1929. The island is named after Alexander Parris,

once an owner of the island and the public treasurer of South Carolina in the 1700s. It encompasses approximately seven thousand eight hundred acres and is connected to the mainland over a small series of causeways leading to the main bridge. Traditionally, all Marines east of the Mississippi River are trained here.

Basic recruit training has five steps: Receiving—when the recruit first arrives on the Island, before he is assigned to a platoon; First Phase—when he is introduced to the basic military protocol and subjects; Second Phase—when the recruit goes through the rifle range for weapons training; Mess and Maintenance—when the recruit spends time on KP duty and in the grounds and base maintenance group; and the final phase—when each recruit must prepare himself, through tests and inspection, for his graduation from the Island. Throughout all five steps, the recruit is continually involved in a rigid schedule of diet, rest and physical training necessary to meet the standards set up by the Marine Corps. Its policy has always maintained that each recruit will receive the most thorough and most exacting training available. Each recruit leaves basic training with the knowledge that he has completed what has been called the toughest recruit training in the world.

II

RECEIVING

II

IT WAS A HOT LATE June morning, marked already with
sweat from the early P.T., the Marines' abbreviated term for
physical training. They have a way of converting everything into
their own image on Parris Island, or in the Corps language, the
Island. Our entire "series" (a company or more of men) was
standing at attention, each platoon posed rigidly, waiting as the
colonel walked out in front of the assembly. He turned and
faced us full forward with that Marine Corps look of
authority—cold, uncaring eyes that both looked at you and
through you.

"This Island will be the closest we hope you will ever come to
living under a communistic government," he began. He pur-
posefully hesitated here, looking to one side and then slowly,
ever so slowly, looking over the entire series before continuing.
He had our attention. No doubt about that. After his calculated
silence he continued, "Here on the Island we do our own laun-

dry, and I don't mean the soap and water kind." Yep, he had our attention. All you had to do was to squint from the corners of your eyes at the three hundred or so recruits to see that he had our undivided attention. The speech continued for another thirty or forty-five minutes, with the colonel's telling us what the Marine Corps expected of us, and what we in turn could expect from the Corps. I remember more of that speech than I really care to. Phrases like "We will do the thinking for you—all you have to do is what you're told, when you're told," and "for the next thirteen weeks we're the only family you've got," and on and on.

"Oh hell," I thought. "What am I doing here?" I could sense that I wasn't the only recruit with that sober thought. Each recruit was having to deal with the colonel's comments in silence, since our DI, or drill instructor, had already emphasized that we talked only when we were instructed to. In the week since we had arrived, I don't recall our having been instructed to say much of anything except our name.

It might be best to fill you in on the first week's activities here so you can appreciate our desperation even before the colonel's speech. I am from Charleston, about seventy-five miles north of Parris Island. I left Charleston for the Island on June 19 by Greyhound bus with two other recruits. I knew them both; we looked forward to going through training together. It was early that morning that I left home and picked up my fiancée, Kathy, to drive me to the bus station. I had kissed her good-bye and was somewhere out on Highway 17 before the reality of what I was doing hit me. It was going to be Salvo, Miller and me against the world. That's O.K., though, I thought, we could handle that.

We arrived in Beaufort about an hour and a half later. Other recruits were milling around the bus station, waiting for someone who knew what to do next. I had not eaten breakfast, so I went into the small cafe next door and ordered a hamburger and chocolate shake. This was on the recommendation of the short order cook after he heard I was bound for the Island. As it turned out, he knew his business. I didn't see another hamburger or chocolate shake until I graduated from the Island on September 10. After the quick snack, we sat around the bus station and exchanged names with some of the other recruits waiting to go with us.

Shortly, a long green Marine Corps bus pulled up to the curb and a crisp, snappy Marine Corps sergeant stepped off. I suppose we all wanted to see ourselves looking as he did—sharp creases in the dress blue pants with the wide crimson band down the legs; wide white webbed belt with the big rectangular brass buckle sporting the Corps emblem, polished so bright it seemed to emit its own light; the tan dress shirt with rifle and pistol expert badges and several ribbons above them over the left breast pocket, and dark green sergeant's stripes on the sleeve. He wore a white Marine Corps dress hat, again with the shiny brass eagle, globe and anchor square on the front. I had never seen such a shine on a pair of shoes! They weren't patent leather, either. It was a real Marine Corps spit shine that I knew must have taken hours and hours. One of the few. The Proud. The Marines. Yes, sir, that was going to be us before long. Where do I start? Just show me what to do to look like that. Straight off the poster.

He calmly called out our names and checked off each as we climbed aboard. The six- or seven-mile trip out to Parris Island passed quickly as we laughed and joked with one another. The sergeant sat strangely quiet up front as we shared cigarettes and names. The stop at the gates to the Island was only a brief delay in our trip, but as soon as we had passed, the bus pulled off the righthand side of the road and stopped. Our poster Marine stood up and turned to face us. In a voice that rocked both the bus and our souls, he addressed us in a less-than-human tone.

"All right," he bellowed, "Shut your fucking mouths and put out the smokes. You're on Marine Corps land now and you'll do it the Corps way from now on. You sit straight and keep your mouths shut till you're spoken to. Spit out any gum, and if any one of you lights up another smoke, you'll eat the son-of-a-bitch. You got that?"

The shocked silence on the bus should have let the sergeant know we understood—fully. Our picture-perfect Marine had turned into a mad, screaming monster, all in the few seconds it had taken to pass through those well-landscaped gates still visible through the rear windows of the bus. Evidently he had never heard that "Silence gives consent" because he repeated the question even louder. "You got that?" he bellowed, the veins on the sides of his neck bulging out thick and strong.

His loud repetition jolted some of us back to a state of semiconsciousness, so we meekly replied, "Yes, Sir." Not all of the recruits had responded, and our reply had seemed to anger the monster in uniform even more.

"I can't hear you!" he thundered.

"Yes, sir!" we screamed all together and as loudly as we dared try. Anything to calm down the monster, to keep him at bay until his sanity returned. Maybe the heat of the day was too much, or maybe it was his job, but whatever the reason, settle the monster down.

"Now," he continued in his stormy rage, "close the windows and listen up." We immediately closed the windows and turned anxious eyes back toward the front of the bus. "From now on, you'll say 'Sir' to anything that grows on this island except another recruit. That will be the first word out of your mouth each and every time you speak, and you don't speak unless you're told to do so by someone other than a recruit. You hear me?"

"Sir, yes, Sir!" we screamed again.

The monster looked down at the Marine Corps driver and nodded his head, then turned square towards the back of the bus, his arms folded across his chest as the bus eased back out onto the road. I was sitting near the rear and turned to see the gates slipping away behind us. A sickening, empty knot in my stomach told me what I already suspected, that all was not well.

A thundering, mad-dog rage from the monster up front quickly brought me back to the present as I realized he was talking—no screaming—at me. "What in hell are you doing?" he bellowed. Before I could even start to reply, he tore in again.

"Didn't I just tell you to sit straight? Does that mean look around? Hell, no, it doesn't! It means keep your head and eyes straight ahead! Your fucking ears quick working? You can't follow directions? What's your name, Maggot?" All these questions in a full battle-crazed rage as he made way to the back of the bus. "My name is . . . " He cut me off in an even louder rage with "What's the first word out of that mouth? Didn't I just tell you what it is supposed to be? You forgot that, too?"

"Sir, my name is Moore," I answered.

"That's closer to it, Moore! You'd best get your act together if you expect to make it in this man's Corps," he continued, still in the frenzied rage. "Now sit down and shut your face!"

He spun on his heels and retraced his steps to the front of the bus, where he turned, planted his feet firmly and continued standing with his arms folded across his chest, sternly watching over his fresh charges. "Great!" I thought. "Just great! I haven't been more than three hundred yards past the gate and I've already had my first encounter with the way of the Corps." Had I known, really known, that this was only the tip of the iceberg, I'd probably have gone down like the *Titanic* and asked for a Section 8 (the Army term for the discharge of a mental case).

We rode on in silence for the mile or two to the Receiving Center for recruits. We rode silently past the statue of the flag-raising on Mt. Suribachi on Iwo Jima. It was on our left, close beside the road and in front of the parade ground where we would, upon completion of our basic training, graduate under the watchful eyes of the men on that statue. On we rode, past the base theater and groups of brick buildings with the various offices needed to house and staff recruit training on the Island. Past the statue of Iron Mike, an early Marine holding ammunition and a machine gun over one arm and a pistol high over his head in the other hand, erected in memory to all those passing through the Island who were killed in the country's various wars.

When the bus pulled up in front of a brick, two-story building marked "Receiving," we found three more monsters waiting to scream and guide us into the structure and into the proper classroom for the next set of instructions. They must all have been graduates of the same special school that turns perfectly normal-looking people into hideous, screaming animals. Either that, or the Marine Corps had found a way to make all these raging animals look, on the surface, like normal people.

The monsters had us turn in all our civilian personal property next. This included electric shavers, after shave lotion (I never could figure that out, unless they thought we might drink it!), watches (they have their own time on the Island), wallets and pictures (there went my whole identity), and any other glass or breakable items, along with any jewelry. The only items we were left with were the clothes on our backs, which would also be taken in the next few days. All this confiscated personal property was then mailed back home to a "person or persons you so deem." We reluctantly but quietly parted with each item as instructed by the monster in charge.

It amazed me to see all these bullies running us here and there, always mad and never pleased with any of our actions even though we tried with all our might to follow their orders as best we could. It seemed that the whole Island was overpopulated with the raging animals who could be calmed down only when they were off together, in small clusters, among their own kind. At such times you would see them smile at one another, speak in a normal tone and practice "being normal." This, I guess, was so that the population around the small town of Beaufort wouldn't suspect their real identity when they got a pass into town for a night of drinking and having a little fun on their own. We would watch them as we quietly ate our own hurried meals in the mess hall over the next two days.

Those two days were filled with completing all the written facts that would become the nucleus of the personal file that the U.S. Government kept on us all. I answered all the questions as honestly as I could, and since our monster had told us to answer *all* questions, I either guessed or lied about the ones I didn't know how to answer. Like the question of whether there had ever been a history of mental illness in my family. I had never thought about asking my parents that one, and they never volunteered that there had or had not been such a history. I think I must have lied when I answered "No" on that one. Surely there must be mental illness somewhere in there. After all, I was on the Island, and no sane person would volunteer to do that, would he?

I was born in Augusta, Georgia, on the eighth of January 1943, the middle child; I had an older sister, Patricia, and younger brother, Bill. Both of my parents' families were from rural backgrounds and I have always felt a gentle tug towards the outdoors and the quieter ways of life in the country. My early school memories bring to mind strict teachers and plenty of homework, a task I did not enjoy. My family moved to Charleston after World War II, and my father was employed by the railroad industry. Sports played an important role in my life, and I was fortunate to possess the skills to participate. My love for sports carried over into high school and college, and I remained in touch with the outdoors through hunting and fishing as time would allow, although I never felt I had adequate time to devote to these pleasures. I held part-time jobs throughout my high school days and was the proud owner of a 1950 Plymouth sedan. I had paid a high ransom of $75.00 for that symbol of independence, and it was one of my best investments.

I had had visions of being a Marine for years, and so it seemed only logical for me to enlist in the Corps. I was 5'10" and weighed 165 pounds, so it is obvious that I was not considered to be of extraordinary size in the eyes of the Corps. Since the Marines do not take much stock in a man's size, only his ability to complete a task at hand, I was secure in the knowledge that I had made the right decision. At least before the experiences of the last two days. At any rate, we completed the task of filling out all the forms, and listened to all the lectures and screaming of the monsters, meekly following all orders and wishing for a way to turn back the clock—or turn it forward.

On the second day, at one or two o'clock in the morning, we were sitting at the position of attention—the only way a recruit was allowed to sit—waiting for more instructions from the growling monsters pacing back and forth in front of the class, when the swinging double doors from the hall on our right exploded open as though a truck had somehow found its way up to the second floor and smashed the doors to splinters. At the sound, all eyes turned, quickly trying to assess which direction the runaway truck would take. To our astonishment, there was no truck, not even a compact car—only three more monsters. But these dressed differently and looked even fiercer than the monsters we were becoming used to.

Nineteen years later, I can still see those three DIs, our drill instructors, standing in their feet-spread-arms-folded-across-chests stance, three abreast, looking invincible and unmoving in their stone hard stares as they looked us over. A pregnant silence was followed by the raging, screaming, staccato voices of the three new monsters as they ordered us outside and had us form into four lines, each with ten or twelve men, one behind the other, spaced approximately an arm's length apart. Each DI ran about screaming and raging as they "instructed" us on how to assume the position of attention. You could hear the different voices individually, while at the same time blended together as they yelled. "Head and eyes straight to the front, you maggots!" "Feet at a 45-degree angle, you dumbass!" "What the hell are you doing, Private?" "Did I tell you to move? Then why in hell are you moving?" "What's your name, Maggot?" "Well, you'd best square your ass away, Miller!" "Suck in that gut, you shithead! Suck it in! More!" On and on it went for another ten minutes or so, over and over. The harassment eventually began to ease off some and the shortest of the three monsters ordered us to face left. Needless to say, we faced left.

"My name is Sergeant Egge and I'm your Senior Drill Instructor," was the first sentence he said to us as a group, "And these are your junior drill instructors, Corporal Rast and Corporal Thomson." As the senior DI, Egge would be the responsible noncommissioned officer in charge of Platoon 340. Each platoon had one senior DI, and two junior DIs who were working their way through the ranks to become senior DIs with platoons of their own later. He paced (they all paced as they talked) relentlessly back and forth in front of us. His uniform was the same as that of all the other monsters we had encountered except that it fit better and looked crisper. The shoes were even brighter and he wore a smooth, black belt at his waist. The other two wore the wide, webbed cartridge belt. Square in the middle of the back of their belts hung a three- by five-inch first aid pack, and their buckles were the large rectangular brass ones with the Marine Corps emblem, much the same as what of the sergeant who had met us at the bus station at Beaufort.

This description is not sufficiently complete for you to see what I saw as I watched Egge pace before us, but I can try to complete the picture for you. The one thing I haven't described is the singular item that has pushed men to their limits through generations and generations of Marine Corps tradition. It signifies all that Parris Island stands for, and is, in reality, what Parris Island is about. The "Smokey-the-Bear" hat. The campaign cover. It is respected to almost irrational reverence in the Corps. The Corps gives nothing away; it's always earned, and it's always paid for, with interest, before anything is awarded. That hat, too, must be earned and the price paid—three times over. Attending drill instructors' school takes enormous strength and enough mental and emotional stress to destroy most people. Marines know what it takes to get "the hat," and accordingly, respect the man it shades.

After Sergeant Egge had finished telling us who the DIs were, he informed us we were going to get our first Corps issue of clothing and then head for "the barn," Egge's term for our barracks, home for the next twelve weeks. The next hour or so was a blur of activity as we got our heads sheared, received clothing and were issued our official Marine Corps boots. All the clothes issued were tossed into a seabag and we stood in formation, under the watchful eye of one of the DIs, until all recruits were assembled. Somewhere inside the building were the remains of our contact with individuality. We certainly didn't look like military men, with our boots, utility (combat) trousers, and T-shirts, standing together in a rag-tag formation, holding our seabags strapped over one shoulder. But we didn't look like civilians either, with our clean-shaven heads, and all dressed alike. We were more like a group of tadpoles whose legs have appeared—no longer looking like a fish, but certainly a long way from becoming a frog.

We started toward our new home in a rough formation, trying vainly to keep in step with the cadence barked loud and clear by Egge. It was a losing battle for the DIs, but they ran back and forth, trying to get first one recruit, then another, in step. Some individuals were able to keep in step, but as a group we were a total mass of confusion.

In what I'm sure was a planned maneuver, our path to the barn carried us on the back streets between old, two-story, pre-World War II wood frame buildings covered with the slate grey asbestos shingle siding. Huge water and steam pipes crossed overhead, all with a new coat of silver paint. The summer heat was in full force and we all sweated enough to please the monsters as we trudged along.

We passed within eyeshot of other recruit platoons who had been on the island long enough to master the skills of close-order drill. Each time we came close enough, the older platoon's DI would sound off louder in his own song of cadence and his charges proudly strutted by all stiff and straight, leaning back with their new-found skill, showing off for the rag-tags.

After a quarter-mile march, we came to some new three-story brick buildings. To our surprise, Egge turned us toward the oak tree-shaded area directly in front of one of the well manicured structures. Each of these barracks was rectangular, the side with the shorter dimension facing the road. In single file, he led us to the second floor and proclaimed this to be our home. As we entered, I noticed the painted concrete floor, and roll-out casement windows running the length of the building. There were two rows of bunk beds, one down each side, but pulled out from the wall far enough to permit walking space between the end of the bunks and the wall. That left a clear corridor about ten feet wide down the center of the barracks. Two footlockers, called locker boxes, were under each of the steel framed bunk beds, and the bare mattress was folded in half with a pillow on top, a signal that the last occupants had no intention of returning.

We filed in and were told to line up in front of the bunks, starting from the far end. We were issued sheets, a blanket, wash cloth, towel and pillow case. The DIs screamed fast, short orders to put our gear in the correct place. They explained the Marine Corps procedure for making up a bunk, demonstrating how a coin really would bounce on it if it were made up properly. We practiced over and over, never pleasing the monsters who would inspect the bunks and then scream about how each of us appeared to have some problem that prevented us from being able to handle even this simple task. His dissatisfaction expressed, the DI would rip the cover off the bunk and order us to make it again. These fun and games continued for another forty-five minutes or so and the sweat ran freely. There, of course, was no air conditioning in the barracks, and there were no breezes stirring; the air was stale and humid.

After the Marine Corps bed-making instructions, we were taken outside and formed again in our column of fours, this time between the buildings rather than out front along the road where an occasional car would pass about a hundred feet from the building.

We later found out we were assigned to the Third Recruit Training Battalion, one of three such battalions on Parris

Island. To orient you somewhat, the First Battalion is on the lefthand side of the main road as you approach the parade field behind the flag raising monument of Iwo Jima. The barracks for the First Battalion are on the opposite side of the parade ground from the monument. Directly across the street from the monument is the Second Battalion, separated from the road by another smaller, paved parade area used for their close-order drill and practice. Both the First and Second Battalion barracks were constructed at the same time as the other pre-World War II structures we had marched behind on the way to our barracks.

The Third Battalion was called "Disneyland" because of the newer brick barracks, and because we were separated from the other two battalions by about a quarter of a mile. We were not even in sight of the main parade ground, and appeared to be somewhat isolated from the rest of the inhabitants of the Island. I suppose that, too, helped support their image of a Disneyland. We later learned there was a price to pay for living in Disneyland, a price that the other two battalions wouldn't have wanted to pay merely to live in those newer barracks.

Back to the description of my new home. The Third Battalion was off to the right of the main road passing in front of the main parade ground. There were six identical barracks spaced about thirty feet apart. Behind the barracks was a paved parade deck (area) approximately one hundred yards by three hundred yards. At the back of our barracks and looking across the parade deck were the Battalion command officers, fronting up to the other side of the parade area. As you looked towards the left, but beside the command buildings, there were an additional three barracks. At the left end of the rectangle was the mess hall, a single-story brick building almost as long as the width of the parade deck. At the other end of the three-hundred-yard length of the rectangle, to your right, were various classrooms and storage buildings, as well as the chapel. All of these were old wood frame structures or metal Quonsett huts.

A service road ran behind the mess hall, and across that road

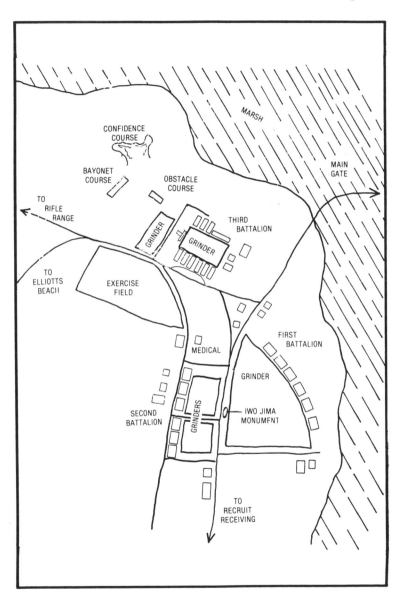

was another small paved parade ground, beyond which was the obstacle course, bayonet course and confidence course. Directly across the road in front of our barracks was a huge, green grass-covered exercise field, with some structures we would later use in our physical training exercises. Between our barracks and the road was a row of stately live oak trees with widespread, low-hanging limbs. To anyone other than a recruit undergoing basic training, these might give an appearance of tranquility.

The trip over to the mess hall that first afternoon was a repeat of the trip from the Recruit Receiving to our barn, with Egge's calling cadence and Thomson's and Rast's running around and through the platoon, yelling and screaming all the way. We were instructed to move sideways at the position of attention while holding out our standard military metal food tray. Older recruits heaped foot on each man's tray as he passed in file through the food line. Each of us would follow the man in front of him until we filled a twelve-man table, six men to each bench, then stand at attention while one man said grace. The blessings for the food were printed on a plastic-coated card which had its own little stand on each table, much like that for the dessert menu or wine list in restaurants. The recruit who said grace could choose to read any one of the six or eight short blessings on the card. Upon completion of this ritual, all twelve men were to sit, at the same instant and as one, to start eating. It was a favorite game of the DIs to make each table stand up again, yell "Seats!" and have us practice hitting the bench with a single sound. This little game would sometimes be repeated six or seven times before the DI would turn and walk away, signaling acceptance that you had, at least, made a passable attempt at the maneuver.

Let me point out here and now that I found that the tales about lousy food in the military simply didn't apply to Parris Island. Maybe it was because we were worked so hard that any food tasted good, or maybe it was because food was the one creature comfort that the Marine Corps couldn't take from us, but I'll say one thing about the food: It was damned good! I'll also say something else about it. The Marine Corps piled it high, not holding back unless the recruit was on a diet, prescribed by the base medical staff after our physicals.

We remained seated as a group until the DI yelled "340 . . . Outside!" Platoon 340 was our official recruit platoon number. On that command, in single file and one table at a time, we would empty the remains from our tray, put it on a metal counter and rigidly march back outside to form another formation for the return march to the barracks.

After several meals there would be a new procedure for leaving the mess hall. The DI on duty instructed us that we would be at the position of attention outside in our regular platoon formation by the time the DI had finished eating. The DI on duty would get his food after the last man in the platoon had filled his tray. We then ate in hurried silence, glancing toward the DI's table to see that we were making satisfactory progress toward getting outside before he finished.

We were also instructed that we would eat all food on the tray prior to leaving the mess hall. There were occasions when one of the last recruits in line did not finish in time. He would be stopped by one of the DIs as he hurried to put up his tray and be chewed out for not having following instructions. On occasion the DI would have the recruit set the tray on the counter, and then shove his face in the remaining food to eat it like an animal. Needless to say, it took only a few lessons like this to teach us to be outside and waiting when the DI finished eating. If you were unlucky enough to be at the end of the line, you had to take less food and eat faster to accomplish this feat. Everywhere we went we were in some type of formation, at attention and under the supervision of one of the DIs.

When we got back to the barn, one of the junior DIs went to pick up the extra recruits who would be assigned to Platoon 340, and shortly we had about seventy-five men in the barracks, enough for our full contingent under Marine Corps standards. We would have to wait until the three other platoons in our company were filled in to start our full training schedule together. That took another couple of days, during which time we trained as a company. I found there is fierce competition and rivalry among the platoons to be the best at each phase of training. We were instructed to pay no heed to the "scumbags" who weren't lucky enough to have gotten into 340. I never, while on Parris Island, met any of the recruits of our series (that's what the Marine Corps called the Company), even though I knew their faces from the daily joint classes and training sessions.

The very first night on Parris Island started out with lessons from the DIs on hygiene and all the personal things the Corps expected you to do to meet its standards. Everything from how to bathe to how to shave. We were assured by Egge that our DIs would tell us when to do each and in what order each would be done. We were then "instructed" to write a letter back home and "instructed" to tell them that we were fine and would write again soon. We handed the letters to the DIs, who read each letter, then instructed the writer to seal it and put it on the table to be mailed.

The whole platoon was now, as I've said, together in our barn, all of us with a common frightened look of despair. All three DIs alternated between sitting at a table (placed in the center aisle at one end of the rows of bunks, but facing back towards the entrance from the street) and walking up and down the squad bay, the Corps name for that section of the barn where we lived. The recruits on one side of the squad bay would shower and shave while those on the other wrote letters and had them approved. We would switch tasks when ordered to do so by the DI. This pattern would be repeated daily until we left the Island, the only difference being that the time when you weren't in the shower would not always be spent writing letters home, as we would soon find out.

To help orient you about our home for the next three months, I'll describe our barracks' interior. You recall our barracks were three story and rectangular, approximately thirty-five feet wide

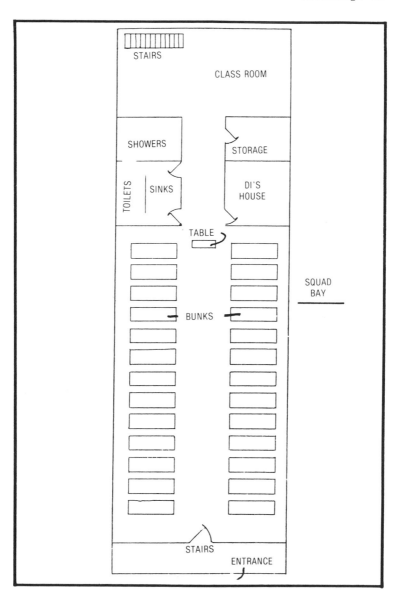

and one hundred feet long, with the narrow width facing the road. Our squad bay was on the second floor, the main entrance door on the street side of the building. The staircase was of concrete and steel, encased in the brickwork of the building itself but open on the street side. From the road, one could see anyone moving up or down the stairs, but only from about waist up and only as he reached the landings where the doorway entrance to each floor was. Between each floor was another landing encased in solid brick. A recruit on either of these landings could not be seen from the street, of course. The first sixty feet or so of the squad bay, entering from the street side entrance, was filled with double decker bunks, approximately twenty on each side. The center aisle, formed by the bunks on each side, was about ten feet wide.

At the foot of the center aisle where the two rows of bunks ended, a hallway about twenty feet long was formed by two rooms on either side of the barracks at this point. On the left were the toilet and showers, while on the right were the DI's house, or room, and a storage room. Following the ten-foot hallway formed by these rooms, the building opened back up to its full width for another twenty feet or so, forming a classroom with storage cabinets along one wall. I don't recall there being any furniture in that back room other than a standard military-grey, four-legged table and a straight-back metal chair with padded seat, back and armrests. A staircase in that room led downstairs and was used by the DIs, but it was "off limits" to recruits. Another door in this room led out to a concrete deck at the back. This was the roof of the series commander's office, a twenty-foot addition at the back of the first floor of the barracks. The deck had a freshly painted steel handrail around its perimeter. I recall being on that deck only once; no, make that twice. Once when Egge decided we needed to watch an older series go through a drill competition and the other when I was there with a photographer and Rast.

The DI's house inside the squad bay opened onto the hallway, but had a large window about four feet high and eight feet long which looked out over the bunks toward the street. Other than several wall lockers, a bunk, file cabinets, desk and chair, there was little else in the room. It seemed as though even the DIs had no personal belongings there. I don't recall seeing any signs of their activities when outside those walls. Even their coffee cups were standard mess hall issue, confiscated at one time or another. Their "house" was the picture of Marine Corps discipline, with everything in its proper place, cleaned and polished. The room looked cold and sterile, as though the occupants used it minimally, only long enough to sleep a little or to sit at the desk to complete the unending stream of paperwork. The window overlooking the squad bay had blinds, and more often than not they were closed.

On either side of the squad bay, behind each row of bunks, were full rows of windows about thirty inches up from the floor and continuing almost to the ceiling. They were the roll-out type, so that when opened, rain couldn't come in but breezes could.

There were screens on the inside—screens that we scrubbed often enough to have darn near worn out the metal. During all the time we were on the Island, we closed those windows only when we moved to the rifle range for three weeks and when we were given "incentive" training. I'll explain that later. Each window section was about thirty inches wide, and when we scrubbed the screens, we also had to wash and polish the glass, inside and outside. In the Corps, window glass must be clean enough to appear invisible. Any dirt or lint in or around the corners was first wiped away with a dry cloth, then brushed with a small paintbrush or a toothbrush, washed, dried and then inspected. Of course, we usually had to repeat the cleaning process numerous times before receiving an approving nod from the monsters.

On our trek from Recruit Receiving, we had been taken to a small base exchange for an initial issue of personal items such as shaving cream, razors, razor blades, bath soap and powder, toothbrush, toothpaste, etc. We were not given the luxury of after shave lotions, cigarettes or even a choice of name brands of toiletries. Each was given a bucket issue with the "necessities" already inside. So much for freedom of choice.

We had finished our showers and letter writing to loved ones that first night when Egge stood on top of the table at the head of the squad bay and gave us the night duty rules. We would have a fire watch—someone awake on two-hour shifts in the squad bay all night. A roster would be posted and we would alternate turns throughout the entire three months. Training would begin before first light, yet we were told to "enjoy the entire night's sleep." He had us stand at attention, after which we would all bend down and touch our toes; then, starting on Egge's left, the first recruit would snap back to the upright position of attention and proclaim loudly, "One, Sir!" The next recruit would repeat the process, yelling "Two, Sir!" and so on down one side and back up the other until everyone sounded off. This ritual, the Marine Corps' method of making sure everyone was accounted for nightly and first thing each morning, continued twice daily up through the morning we left Parris Island.

After counting off in this manner for Egge, we stood rigidly at the position of attention beside our bunks awaiting further instructions. All three DIs were silently patroling up and down the squad bay during the counting off, and now Egge assumed the spread-legged monster stance, frowning as he barked, "Prepare to mount!"

We had to repeat all orders in unison and at the top of our lungs, so we responded, "Prepare to mount. Aye, aye, Sir!" Egge snarled, "I can't hear you!" Hell, we knew that was coming, so we literally tried to shake the building with a repeat performance, "Prepare to mount. Aye, aye, Sir!" With a half smirk, Egge then instructed us loudly, "Ready . . . Mount!"

That was our cue, and you can believe we hit those bunks as instructed. As usual, though, we had not done it "as one" and had to repeat the exercise four or five times. Each time we fell into bed we had to lie at the position of attention until Egge yelled either "At Ease!" or "Again!" That first night while we lay rigidly in our bunks, facing straight up as though we had been standing at attention and simply fallen back onto the bunk, Egge again gave us a short talk on Marine Corps history and discipline. When he finally gave the command "At Ease!" we were more than ready to be rid of the monsters and alone with our thoughts, even if it would be for only a few hours.

Egge walked back up the squad bay to the door to the DI's house, where the light switch was located. A large galvanized metal trash can was situated by the last bunk before the narrow hall began, and Egge gave it a sharp crack with his fist as he passed, just to let us know that even when it was time to rest it was no time to relax. When he reached the light switch, he turned to give a final, stern Marine Corps frown toward the recruits before he hit the light switch to engulf us in blackness. "Sleep, Maggots!" were his last words of wisdom for the day.

The dark room was a quiet, welcomed friend after the constant yelling and harassment of the monsters that day. I remember that night vividly even after all this time. The luxury of cooling off in the showers had already become a fuzzy memory, replaced by the humid, oppressive heat of night. The sweat had started again even before we finished drying off after the shower, and by now we were soaked even as we lay in the solitude of darkness with the windows full open. Somewhere off in the night came the lonesome sound of taps played on a recording into a microphone and amplified through outdoor speakers, the military's method of saying good night to its own.

Unfamiliar to me were the occasional coughs and the constant squeaks of the bunks' metal springs as each recruit searched for the best sleeping position. I had never slept in a room with seventy men before, yet the sounds were oddly comforting. Maybe they assured me that I wasn't as alone as I felt right then, and I can say for a fact that I was as lonely then as I had ever been in my life. Here I was, with seventy new faces, condemned to spend three months of my life under the thumbs of monsters who displayed not even a hint of humanitarianism. A feeling of despair crept up slowly as I lay there that night. Surely they couldn't, or wouldn't, keep up the same treatment for three months!

Off to my left I heard the quiet sniffle of someone's crying in his bunk, thinking that others around him were sleeping. I did what I could for him by pretending to sleep, giving him as much privacy as one could under the circumstances. I never found out who was crying. I tried to eliminate possible candidates as I knew the perpetrator had to be within four or five bunks of mine. The quiet crying continued nightly for almost two weeks and then stopped altogether. I felt relieved that whoever it was had finally come to grips with his fears.

There are those who will feel no emotion about that recruit's nightly battles, but they were real; and there simply was no other outlet, nor anyone to discuss his problems with. Crying would have been seen as a weakness by the monsters, and you always had to be alert to keep any hint of weakness away from their ever-watchful eyes. Most of us felt the same as he in the quiet night after the lights were turned off; each was left in his own inner world of thought; and each of us had to fight the battle alone. I felt close to him, whoever the anonymous fighter was, for in witnessing his nightly encounter with himself, I had shared his fears and apprehension.

As the first night grew older, I remember the soft glow from the bathroom light which cast a shadow down the squad bay. Though the heat was intense and no breeze was blowing, I pulled the sheet up to my chest, and remember vaguely the sounds of crickets and thoughts of cold beers and fast cars, of air conditioning and television, of pretty girls and parties . . . .

III

GUARDIAN ANGELS

S ERGEANT EGGE. ABOUT 5'10" and about 175 pounds. I couldn't tell you the color of his hair; he kept it cut skin close. Clear, knowledgeable eyes with a healthy sparkle were set in a stone chiseled face. He had a square chin and thin lips through which would later pass a quiet, normal and pleasant voice when explaining some important facts on a one-on-one basis, but also a voice capable of summoning up all the gravel and rage from the bowels of hell when someone screwed up. Physically, he was cold-rolled steel. His muscles showed clearly through his uniform, with ripples and bulges from hard work and exercise. This man had to be here. He exuded the Corps image of the DI. We knew he was tough and exacting, and figured that if we tried to cut this man with a straight razor, all we'd get would be a dull blade. He had broad shoulders and a tanned, healthy glow to his skin. He wore his DI hat cocked slightly lower in front than most other DIs, and seemed to have eyes and ears incapable of missing the slightest movement or sound from any direction.

When we were first introduced to our senior DI, it was, of course, a verbal introduction, so there was no doubt how to pronounce his name. It is an odd name, not one you see everyday. It is pronounced just like the word "egg", then put the sound of long e at the end. Two syllables, and you've got it: Egg-e.

Egge could probably be described as the typical DI on Parris Island. He was demanding, to be sure, and he could summon the monster at will when we didn't perform to his expectations. But there was another side of Egge that we were permitted to meet from time to time. That side would surface when 340 performed a maneuver well. Egge couldn't hide his satisfaction like Rast and Thomson. He sometimes would jump in excitement and yell, "That's it! That's it! Damn it, you've got it!" Then, there were less enthusiastic times, some of them dictated by his personal moods, when we'd hear him simply reply, under the same circumstances, "Good! . . . Good! . . . Now, let's do it again!" This time we saw approval, but not the excitement.

DIs could be compared to another group of people most of the public can identify with: youth league baseball coaches. Some DIs, as some of those coaches, were very stoic in their approach to their task. Those DIs either couldn't or wouldn't expose their feelings about our performance even when they were pleased. Maybe they felt it would be a sign of weakness to express unchecked joy; I'm not sure. But with such DIs, we were hard pressed to know when they were pleased with our accomplishments. Rast and Thomson fit into this category.

Other DIs, just as other coaches, were enthusiastic and excitable when they were pleased. They reminded me of the coach who, when one of his kids hits a home run, jumps from the bench to greet him when he crosses home plate, patting him in genuine jubilance, sharing in the joy of accomplishment. He is happy, and doesn't care who witnesses his joy. Egge was that kind of DI.

Egge talked out of one side of his mouth when he was mad, and also when he called cadence. While we marched, Egge would usually be off to one side or the other about two-thirds of the distance towards the last of the ranks. He would cock his head slightly to one side when the command was to be a thundering boom, and his chin would tuck in towards his chest ever so slightly. He wore his trousers about an inch higher on his waist than Rast or Thomson, and because of his height, or lack of it, had to extend his legs fully to achieve the thirty-inch military stride.

When 340 was just an infant, Egge showed no compassion or mercy in the administration of discipline. He had the ability to detect even the slightest irregularity in a task performed. The perpetrator of that irregularity had to deal with Egge's anger, and his anger was as fierce as a raging hurricane. Egge could do as much with a verbal assault as most DIs could do with physical abuse. When he did use corporal punishment, it appeared to be a controlled attack rather than an anger-filled rage. His fist carried the power of a man twice his size, which I can attest to per sonally.

I'll never know if it was a result of his DI training or a personality trait, but he had an eye for detail. It was a critical eye to start with, but as 340 grew into its adolescence, it became more encouraging than critical. He watched his herd with the knowing eye of a stern taskmaster, and his dedication to the Marines appeared to be as genuine as it was absolute.

I never knew how long Egge had been a DI before coming to 340, and since I never saw him after I left the Island, I never knew how many platoons were in his care after 340. I will give him this much; if you did what he told or showed you, no more, no less, you need have no fear of his wrath. On the other hand, God help you when you screwed up, for the woman scorned hath no fury like the DI unheeded.

Both junior DIs were younger and larger than Sergeant Egge. "Larger" would hardly do justice in describing Corporal Rast. He stood 6'4'' or 6'5'' and would probably tip the scales around 230 or 235 pounds. He had a square face with dark eyes, deep set with a more somber look than Sergeant Egge's. His hands, which I'll go into more detail about later, were huge, hard-muscled appendages which he, probably unconsciously, would swing with the palms facing to the rear when he walked. As one might expect, he had large feet and probably had trouble finding shoes to fit them, as well as uniforms to fit his square torso properly. He was extremely agile for a man his size and could surprise you with his quick bursts of speed and energy, which seemed to lie in check just under the surface.

Corporal Thomson stood about 6' even and probably weighed about 200 pounds. Although not apparent in his family name, his appearance suggested a possible American Indian heritage. His skin was darkish and he had high cheekbones and dark eyes. He had an oval-shaped face with solemn eyes and appeared to be more tuned to the emotional stresses that his charges exhibited. Physically, he was less noticeably muscular than his two associates, but was no less able to match them stride for stride when the occasion called for action. He had a habit of looking first to one side and then to the other as he talked rather than concentrating his attention on the person or persons to whom he was talking. Somehow, he gave the appearance of a teddy bear, but one that you couldn't play with—one you could only look at because of the monster who lived inside.

I never knew if Sergeant Egge was married. Corporal Rast had a wife and the couple lived on base, I recall. Corporal Thomson was also married, and I was told he had children. He, too, lived on base. It seems strange, now that I think back, that I knew so little about the nonmilitary side of those three men who shaped my whole existence for that period of my life. Surely that's part of the Marine Corps training instructions, but it does seem a weak link in their chain. I guess I should have sought further details about those men while I was still in the Corps. The things I learned from them had a profound impact on my life, and yet I know so little of them.

IV

RUDE AWAKENING

IV

I AWOKE THE FIRST MORNING to find Parris Island under attack by some powerful unknown enemy. Brilliant white flashes from exploding shells lit the darkness for an instant, followed by the total blackness of night. Mortar shells exploded in the midst of the squad bay and the DIs ran up and down the center aisle, yelling, attempting to organize the chaos, and obviously trying to tell us to arm ourselves for the fight. Recruits jumped from their bunks, crashing into one another and adjoining bunks as we tried to fight away the cobwebs of deep sleep and find some order to the invasion. Miraculously, the building had not yet collapsed, although it was obviously not going to take all this abuse much longer.

It looked as though Platoon 340 would be killed before the Marine Corps could even issue us rifles.

From out of the confusion a voice boomed, "You'd best get your asses in front of your bunk at the position, Ladies!"

From another direction, "Get up! Get up! Hurry up! Hurry up! Hurry up!"

From still another direction, "You maggots trying to sleep away the whole fucking day?"

Yet another voice, "You'd best snap outta it and get your shit together! It's another glorious day in the Marine Corps, where everyday's a holiday and every meal a banquet! Hurry up! Get a move on! We ain't got all day!"

Well, so much for the invasion of Parris Island. The brilliant flashes from the exploding shells had been Sergeant Egge's flipping the lights off and on repeatedly. The exploding mortars turned out to be the galvanized trash can, kicked down the center aisle, bouncing on the concrete floor and hitting some of the bunks. The lid had come off and rolled in another direction, angrily clattering and rattling on the floor until it came to rest against a locker box halfway down the squad bay. The chaotic scramble had died out by now, and we all stood sleepily at the "position" as the three DIs paced the center aisle, ever watchful for any flaw in our actions.

We went through the counting off procedure again, then were allowed to go to the "head," the all-military name for the restrooms. We got dressed in our utility trousers, combat boots and T-shirts as instructed and stood—again, at attention—awaiting our next set of orders.

"340 . . . Stand by to fall outside!" boomed Egge.

"340 . . . Stand by to fall outside. Aye, aye, Sir!" was our reply.

Egge leisurely walked halfway down the squad bay, hands behind his back, ever looking over each man as he passed, yet with no indication he was taking anything more than a casual stroll. Suddenly he yelled, "Get outside!"

At that we filed out at a dead run to the dark pavement in front of the barracks. We had been instructed enough already in the Marine Corps way to evacuate the barracks; it resembled a wild stampede as we exited the squad bay. Each recruit had been told in very understandable Marine Corps language that the center aisle was off limits. We were never to set foot on the center aisle unless instructed by someone who had earned the title of Marine, which meant someone who had completed basic training.

We had a short run of about a mile to endure in the darkness of the warm June morning, and it passed quickly enough for those of us who thought we were in good physical condition. There were, however, a number of recruits who had reported to basic training overweight and/or not in even respectably decent physical condition. To them, I'm sure the run was pure torture as they stumbled and huffed along. Miller, who had come from Charleston with me and was about twenty or twenty-five pounds overweight, was one of the struggling recruits. I remember the monsters constantly yelling at him to keep up.

The sky was just beginning to display the dark grey of dawn as we returned to the parade deck behind the barracks. Following this we were herded through another meal at the mess hall. Mounds of scrambled eggs were piled high on each tray, along with link sausage, hashed brown potatoes, cereal, toast and grapefruit halves. I've never been a milk drinker, so I took one of the juices and hot coffee to drink. When we first started the mile run, I thought it was foolish to have us outside running before breakfast, but as I silently finished my meal I realized how the run had stimulated my appetite. Also, if we had had to run *after* breakfast, most of us probably would have thrown up what we ate. I was still amazed that the food tasted so good, since all I had ever heard about military food was bad.

After breakfast, it was back to the barn for a "head call"—trip to the john—then we were gathered around the table and instructed by Egge to sit on the floor. Rast and Thomson slowly patrolled around the platoon looking for inattention or nodding heads. I'm putting quotation marks around what Egge told us that morning although I don't know that I'm quoting him verbatim (after all, it has been almost twenty years).

"All right, Ladies," he began, "Let's get a few things

straightened our here and now. You're no longer civilians, and you're damn sure not Marines. Right now, you are nothing but Marine Corps property. You don't come to Parris Island, put in your twelve weeks and then go on to another job as a Marine. There are three ways off this Island. First, you can graduate, which is what the Marines expects you to do. Second is a discharge, which is either on a physical or a mental basis, decided by someone other than yourself. The third way is in a pine box, feet first. If you think you can escape by going over the fence, you'd best be a better man than any who have tried before because none of them made it and lived. This Island can only be reached by the gate you came through, over the bridge. If you're a damn good swimmer, you might make it halfway across the bay toward Beaufort, but no further.

"Now, since you know you're going to be here awhile, I'll tell you this, also. You have to graduate from Parris Island. That means you are required to possess certain skills before you leave. You will be tested both mentally and physically at different stages while you're here. If you fail these tests, you will be set back in training and assigned to a platoon several weeks behind this one in order for you to try again. If you keep fucking up on these tests, you'll be set back again. In the Corps, you can spend your entire enlistment right here on this Island in recruit training. Every Marine goes through here under the same system. When you graduate, it'll be because you earned it, because nobody is going to give you a damn thing."

We were fully attentive to each word he spoke that morning. Fears and apprehension were not being laid to rest, but they were being faced now by each recruit. We listened with somber faces. I had known fellows who had gone through the Island and heard the stories they told, but now this stranger was making it the law.

"Next," Egge continued, "is how we handle the problems. Today starts the first day of your training, and we can take care of the problems one of two ways. The first way is by the books.

The Uniform Code of Military Justice tells how each problem can be solved. What that means is that any time you do something wrong, it will be handled by the laws in the Code. If I find rust anywhere on your rifle or equipment, you'll be reported, written up for office hours (an equivalent to our magistrate court system) and will appear before the company commander. Each and every time that happens, another sheet recording the incident will be placed in your permanent file, subject to review each time you come up for promotion, or make application for a job after your enlistment where you have to furnish a copy of your military record. If you have problems in learning how to handle your rifle, or platoon drilling, even incorrect position, that is a discipline problem and will also be written up for office hours for each offense.

"The second way we can handle the problem is not in the books. We take care of it right here in Platoon 340. You fuck up, and Corporal Rast, Corporal Thomson or myself will decide what punishment is justified. We will then administer that punishment, whether it's doing fifty push-ups or a fist in the stomach, or whatever. Then we forget what happened and get on with the program. No written reports or records of the incident."

Egge paused, looking silently at the upraised faces of the new group of recruits. The pause was long enough to allow us to understand clearly what he said. Then he continued: "The decision on which method we use is going to be decided by you, not Corporal Rast, Corporal Thomson or me, so the three of us are going to step out while you discuss it among yourselves. When we come back, you'll vote and tell us which way you want to go. One thing, though. Whichever way you vote, it must be unanimous. If not, then we'll go by the books. One of you will come knock on my door when you're ready."

With that speech completed, the three DIs retreated to the privacy of the DI's house and closed the door and blinds. The silence that followed for the next few seconds was almost unbearable. We had just been told that we had the responsibility of deciding the disciplinary course of our training. That was a heavy burden to place on seventy recruits who were still frightened and confused at the impersonal manner in which the Corps was treating them. Several comments were made by different individuals; I didn't know them then and can't remember now who spoke up. I do know that the consensus was that any detrimental papers put in our permanent file could do irreversible damage, and we certainly didn't want that cloud in our future. That future seemed far away, but too close for us to want to jeopardize any chances for success.

We discussed the fact that we were open to physical punishment of unknown bounds, which we could not alter. How far would they go to punish us? How drastic was a "fist in the stomach," or was it limited to just that? Would fifty push-ups be the limit? Would it include the possibility of a hundred push-ups? We were much like the wino in the gutter who is picked up, cleaned off and stuck in the board room of a large corporation to establish company policy. We were confused, still under the influence of the wine of the monsters. Like the wino, we couldn't have had knowledge about the ramifications of making a decision so all-encompassing, so we, like him, made the decision which seemed the only alternative a corporate board member should make, and sent to advise the DIs we were ready to vote.

Egge again stood in front of the platoon, silent for a few seconds as Rast and Thomson resumed their quiet patrol around our flanks. "One thing more," he started, "is that this will be the only vote you have here, and there will be no second chance to change policy. If there are any questions before the vote, speak up, now." He paused long enough to assure himself that all understood and there were no questions. Oh, I had many questions, but like most of the rest of the platoon, I felt too insecure at that point to bring them up. "O.K.," Egge continued, "all those who say we go by the book, raise your hands." I cast an anxious eye around to see whose hand would go up. As agreed by all a few minutes before, there was none. "O.K.," said Egge, "all those who want to handle it in 340, stand up." Again, as previously agreed, all of the recruits stood in unison to show Egge we were all in this together, win, lose or draw.

"It's settled, then," Egge replied, "so stand by to fall outside!"

"Stand by to fall outside. Aye, aye, Sir!" we responded.

"Move!" he yelled, and we again raced pell-mell out the door and down the steps.

If we had any misgivings about our decision then, and there were those who did, we would have even more as time wore on. We had voted, freely and democratically, to give dictatorial powers to three men none of us knew. If only we could have known—really known—what was to follow, I'm sure there would have been votes by some of the recruits to go by the book. I don't really know if my vote would have changed or not. There were times in my very near future when I know I would have voted the other way. But I'm getting ahead of myself.

V

INITIAL ISSUE

V

THE NEXT SEVERAL DAYS were crammed with tests and classes on everything from Marine Corps history to health and hygiene. The DIs worked with us hour after hour on close-order drill, teaching us the basic movements in formation. Then hours of exhausting PT where we went through push-ups, jumping jacks, knee-bends, pull-ups, and, one of the worst, the "bend and thrust." I don't even know if there is an official name for that exercise, but I can tell you this much: we probably did no less than six or seven thousand during the course of our stay on the Island.

The only way you'll understand how exhausting this exercise can be is to do it yourself about thirty times. It's simple enough: just stand up straight with feet spread about shoulder width apart. At the count of "One," bend at the waist and touch the floor with your palms down, spread a little wider than shoulder width, and place most of your body weight on your hands. Your legs should still be pretty straight. At the count of "Two," shift all your weight to your hands by rocking slightly forward and kicking your legs straight back until they are fully extended, with only your toes touching the floor behind you. You should now be roughly in the up position of a push-up. On the count of "Three," with your upper body in the same position, spring up with your hips and feet and spread your feet about thirty inches before your lower body weight comes down on them to rest. You are still roughly in the up position of the push-up, only you have your feet spread out. At the count of "Four," reverse the process and bring your feet back together. Now you're back to position number two. At the count of "Five," you return to position Number one. The count of "Six" brings you back standing upright, and one complete exercise is accomplished. Sounds easy, right? Well, do it thirty or forty times in combat boots and gear, then come tell me it's easy and I'll buy you a bus ticket to Parris Island.

On either the third or fourth day, we were herded (notice I don't even imply yet that we can call what we did then marching) over behind the giant parade deck by the Iwo Jima statue to one of the smaller tin-clad buildings which served as a storage warehouse. Here we were issued our 782 gear. Now, 782 gear consists of a webbed cartridge belt with all the combat equipment which hooks to that belt, such as first-aid pack and canteen, a backpack (with all the small webbed buckles and straps which we would later learn to use), entrenching tool (small shovel), bayonet, pancho, half of a two-man tent, a pail which would later serve as a seat while working on personal gear and equipment in the squad bay, and our "chrome dome," the heavy plastic helmet liner worn under the outer steel combat helmet. It was called a chrome dome because it was painted silver to reflect some of the sun's heat away from the head. We were slowly acquiring the necessary items that would help mold us into the finished product of generations of Marines. Each newly acquired piece of equipment was secretly admired and touched as though it held some magical secret waiting to be discovered. Next came the big item, the M-14, our rifle. It, too, was issued from one of the tin-clad warehouses which was used as an armory. I'm no stranger to firearms as I've been an avid hunter and outdoors person for most of my thirty-nine years, but a rifle holds a special place in the hearts of all Marines, whether it be the old Springfield-03, the M-1, the M-14 or the new M-16. His life may depend on how well he knows the capabilities of his rifle, and there's an attachment of attitude, if not emotion, to that piece of forged steel.

We lined up single file and one of the DIs called out each of our names as one of the armorers pulled out another M-14, called off the serial number and recorded it by that individual's name. Then it was handed to the recruit, who ran back outside to the platoon formation. We were given a quick lesson on how to march with our rifles slung over our shoulders, the sling to the front. The rifle was snugly held, perpendicular to the ground, by our right thumb, clasped between the sling and our sweaty bodies. The barrels pointed to the sky and protruded slightly above the tops of our chrome domes. As we marched back to the barn, we stood a little straighter and tried harder to keep in step, as we were now expected to present at least an illusion of organization. I don't know why and wouldn't even attempt to explain any theories, but I still know the serial number of that M-14: 210044.

We were back at the barn with Egge showing us how we would store our 782 gear and hang our rifle on the end of our bunk, when the results of our "democratic" election caught up to me. Two locker boxes were stowed under each bottom bunk, the one toward the center aisle belonging to the recruit on the bottom and the one towards the side aisle belonging to the recruit on the top bunk. The boxes held all our extra clothing and personal gear. Additionally, some of the newly issued 782 gear was to be kept there, so we were instructed to get out the locker box and listen up. During lessons or instructions, the locker boxes were placed side by side in the center aisle, leaving enough room between the bunk and locker box for us to sit on our inverted bucket. That left sufficient room in the center aisle for the DIs to prowl between the two rows of locker boxes to inspect what each recruit was doing. We would take out whatever we were to be working on, close the top and use the closed box as an individual work bench or table. Looking from the DI's table back down the squad bay towards the front door, it gave the appearance of two rows of low, box-like coffee tables set end to end and running down both sides of the center aisle.

Egge had shown us how to hang our rifles on the end of the bunk, facing the center aisle. In my haste to hang it correctly, I made a half-twist in the sling of the rifle. I was sitting on my bucket trying to emulate one of the instructions from Rast on some of the many small belts and buckles in our 782 gear when Egge's monster took over.

"Whose fucking rifle is this?" he bellowed, right behind me.

To be perfectly honest, it scared the hell out of me. I had not even known he was anywhere near. When I saw he was talking about my rifle, I jumped to my feet, snapped to attention and replied in a loud voice, "Mine, Sir!"

"What's your name?" he asked, coming around to face me.

"Private Moore, Sir," I replied.

The monster had complete control of Egge now as he roared, "Who in hell told you to put a half-twist in that fucking sling?" Before I had a chance to reply he continued his tirade. "Did I tell you to do it that way? Did I show you that?" His voice kept getting louder and he was now nose to nose with me, his campaign hat only a fraction of a millimeter from my face. His eyes were on fire and he was enraged at this impossible violation. "You can't do it right? You gotta be different? What the fuck's the matter? Can't you get your shit together?"

His pause gave me an instant to reply, and I answered, "Sir, I didn't notice it was twisted!"

He roared back, "You didn't notice? . . . You didn't notice? What the hell do you think this is, a fucking summer camp?"

"No, Sir!" I answered.

"When I take the time," he replied, "to show you assholes how to do something right, you tell me you didn't notice you did it wrong! How many times do you need to be shown? Ten . . . Twenty?"

"No, Sir!" I answered.

All at once, an explosion hit me in the stomach. I didn't know what had happened since Egge had been so close and I had been watching his wild eyes, so I didn't see him as he balled up his fist, brought back his arm and pounded me just above the belt buckle. The air was forced out of me and I doubled over forward, toward Egge, who moved to one side as I hit the floor. The pain was sharper than from blows I had received before. It was much like the pain I experienced while playing football in high school, as a receiver, when a ball was passed to me and I concentrated on nothing but the ball and got tackled blind-sided by a defender I didn't see. The present pain was worse, though, because there was no padding and it was directed at my vulnerable mid-section.

As I fought what felt like unconsciousness approaching and struggled for air, Egge never let up. He bent over and screamed at my fetal-positioned form on the floor, "You'd best get with the program, Shithead! I got better things to do than babysit a bunch of fuck-offs! You got that, Maggot?"

In a hoarse whisper, I answered, still lying on the concrete floor, "Yes, Sir!"

He fairly roared, "I can't hear you!"

I mustered all the strength I could and answered as loudly as possible, "Yes, Sir!"

His rage had not subsided as he replied, "Then get on your fucking feet and fix that rifle! He turned and walked back toward the DI's table up front, never looking back to see what I would do.

I crawled to the foot of the bunk, stood up and quietly untwisted the sling on the rifle under the stolen glances of concern by my bunkmate and the recruits nearest me. That was my first lesson in Platoon 340 discipline, and you can rest assured that I'll never forget it . . . never.

From that moment on, until I left the Island in early September, I knew that our system would work only as long as the weakest recruit could take this punishment, get back on his feet and try it again. Everyone had seen the punishment I received, and now they could see what Egge had meant when he gave us our second option for disciplinary action, and the race was on. There was no turning back now.

VI

PLATOON
340

VI

W HO SHARED IN THIS RITUAL with me? I don't know
enough details about all the recruits of 340 to provide a profile
of each man. We were a cross section of America east of the
Mississippi since all recruits from this territory are trained at
Parris Island; the remainder are trained at San Diego, California. All levels of society were represented, from high school
dropout to master's degree graduate in mathematics; from extremely wealthy families to dirt poor rural farmers; from short
to tall; black to white; fat to thin; strong to weak.

There was Angione, from somewhere in the Northeast, the
kidder, always ready to smile. And Cahill, tall and somewhat
thin, from New York, streetwise but quiet. One of the smallest
men in the platoon was Palmer, a dark-skinned black who gave
one hundred percent all the time. Willard, from North Carolina,
came from a rural background, always reserved yet always alert.
Downes, Kidwell and Houchins were all from Orlando, Florida,

and all with picture-perfect Florida tans. Patrie, Spanbauer and Mutz came from Wisconsin, none of them quitters, even though Mutz was tall and thin and always had to struggle to do pull-ups. Salvo, Miller and I were from Charleston. Miller didn't graduate from the Island with us, but he kept at it and finally made the grade. Rich was from Boca Raton, Florida, and, along with Downes, I still call him a personal friend and we keep in touch. There was Herlihy, whose father was a prominent national broadcaster, a fact that the DIs didn't know until shortly before we graduated.

Sixty-five of us graduated together, and even though I didn't know them all personally, each of us touched the other in some manner in our common plight during those three months. Some of us would be touched by personal tragedies while on the Island, such as the death of a family member or loved one. Some would suffer the emotional trauma of being set back in training. With each such experience, we all shared the emotions of the affected recruit, and a part of each of us probably remains a part of the other members of 340 even today.

Our training would begin in earnest now. The ritual was seldom changed, beginning with the morning run, then breakfast, morning classes and close-order drill, lunch, more classes and drill in the afternoon, dinner, then more drill and classes in the barn at night, then cleaning and polishing and, finally, bed. The cycle began anew the next morning. The whole sequence was carried on under the watchful eyes of at least two of the three DIs. At night they rotated sleeping in the DI's house, taking us through our schedule twenty-four hours a day, seven days a week.

I remember one of the early days when Egge had us out in the morning about 10:30 or 11:00 o'clock teaching us the basics of close-order drill. Rast was on duty with him that morning and their tempers were running close to the edge as they would position first one recruit, then another, only to find that the one they had just positioned had moved. Egge was barking commands; we were sweating profusely.

"Left . . . Face!" Egge screamed.

At that command, we were to turn ninety degrees to the left, nothing more, just turn and resume the position of attention. During the first few weeks someone would always face the wrong direction, however much he concentrated on the command. True to form, someone faced to the right at Egge's left command.

Egge was furious. "Your other left, Angione!" he screamed as he ran up to the recruit. "What the hell are you doing? Do you know your right from your left?"

"Yes, Sir!" Angione replied at the top of his lungs.

"O.K.," yelled Egge, "hold up your right hand!" Angione did. "Hold out your left hand!" Angione obeyed. "Now can you remember your right from your left?" Angione screamed, "Yes, Sir!"

We tried it over and over, each time Egge or Rast raving in someone's face, letting the monster have free rein. Rast was raving at the recruit behind me, "You dumbass! Can't you do anything right?" as the platoon was marching in a straight column. He continued, not waiting for an answer, "Can't you remember anything? Forty inches back-to-chest! That means the length of your arm, Maggot!" The recruit could only yell back as loudly as possible "Yes Sir!" as he tried his best not to run into Rast. All the while Rast was running around the recruit, yelling and screaming as we marched. Rast kept up the pressure by pressing his face as close as possible to the recruit's head and ears.

Egge continued to call cadence as we marched along, never missing a count, passing out little hints right in tune with the rhythm of the count—"Left...Right...Left...Lean back... Dig in those heels...Strut!...Strut!...Strut! ... Forty inches back-to-chest...Left...Right...Left." We struggled to keep in step in a straight line, even if the spacing between each man wasn't perfect. We had come a long way since we left the initial issue warehouse and passed the senior platoon whose DI strutted his charges for our benefit. We were still working on maneuvers of a platoon in close-order drill, but we were not carrying our rifles during these drills.

We found out how to tell a fresh platoon from an older platoon merely by its platoon flag. A new platoon carried the guidearm (the hand-held flag staff carried by a man marching at the front of the platoon) without a flag. In the middle third of the training, the platoon guidearm held a red flag with yellow platoon numbers. During the final third of training, the same flag was carried but the flag's perimeter was bordered with yellow fringe, or small tassels about an inch and a half long and about the diameter of a pencil lead. That flag identified a senior platoon; and we all dreamed of being senior since that meant only a short time later we would leave this place. Of course, if we watched a platoon marching, we didn't need a flag to tell us its stage of training; it was apparent in its marching skills.

Egge, ever the perfectionist of the three DIs, pushed us to excel in close-order drill. He was demanding and tireless, first explaining each movement, then executing it for us to watch, then putting us to the test—over and over and over. We sweated in the hot June sun, practicing each step of a maneuver, only to have the monsters appear when we made a mistake. Then we'd do it again. And again.

Egge was a brilliant strategist. Just as we were about to drop from exhaustion, he would tactfully have us do a maneuver we had learned fairly well; then he'd jump in the air and scream, "Damn! That's it! Strut! Strut! Strut!" After that small amount of praise we would be ready to walk through Hell behind him. Vince Lombardi must have had the same teacher Egge had. We were pushed to the limit, only to have Egge show us through these phsychological games that we had not even come close. He made us believe there was no limit, there was no impossible. Over and over he had told us, "In the Marine Corps, the difficult we do immediately; the impossible takes just a little longer." It, obviously, wasn't an original quote, but he had us believing its message; and there were times when I felt I did the impossible when it seemed there were simply no reserves left in those strained and overworked muscles. Yet, under his leadership, and yes, even under the monsters' harassment, I found the strength to go further and longer to accomplish some task or goal he set.

These first two weeks were spent getting acclimated to the military methods of talking, acting and thinking, in a manner prescribed by the DIs. The classes were hot and teachers longwinded, and sometimes so boring it was hard to stay awake. Those classes discussed everything from Marine Corps history to how to assemble the .45 caliber pistol. Each class usually had one thing in common with all the other classes: all four platoons in our series were present. All of us, platoons 340, 341, 342 and 343, would be marched single file into the classrooms and stand at attention, by platoon, until our DI gave the command "Ready . . . Seats!" our cue, as in the mess hall, to be seated with a single sound. As Egge and Rast would put it, "I want to hear one butt hit the seat!" Of course, we would have to repeat the process a number of times so the monsters could have their fun.

I remember, about the fourth class we had on firearms, the instructor was late, so the DIs from the four platoons played the "Seats" game, each claiming his herd did better than the others. In this friendly argument among the DIs over who was best, each platoon had to repeat the game for the other platoon's DIs to reevaluate. Someone closed the windows and blinds for privacy, and the game continued. Now the room felt like the main oven in the kitchen of Hell. We would stand, wait for command, then hit the bench. The monster would yell "Again!" and we'd repeat the process. Egge and Rast were on duty that day, and Egge was playing some games of his own with us. Instead of his normal "Ready . . . Seats!" he would yell "Ready . . . ," then pause, and even turn his back and start walking away. Then, in an almost inaudible whisper, he would utter a sound which came out as a soft, soft "Psst," as if he were trying to solicit the attention of a stranger on a street corner. We were expected to be so attentive to each command that when the "Psst" came out, we would react as if he had yelled "Seats!" He would whisper the command so softly that to those in the back of the room it appeared as though we had read his mind and followed his mental command to sit in unison, disciples of the perfect form of Marine Corps discipline. It was decided that 340 had won that round, but the other DIs were issuing threats about "next time." When the instructors finally arrived, they found four platoons of soaking wet recruits in a steaming hothouse. Windows and blinds were opened, and life went on.

VII

SQUAD BAY LIFE

VII

LIFE IN THE SQUAD BAY had taken on a pattern by the second week. We would be awakened at about 4:00 or 4:30, a.m., have count-off, head call, morning run and breakfast, then head into our daily training schedule. At night, after chow and some close-order drill practice, it was back to the barn for cleaning gear, showers and shaves, usually a short class, more cleaning and polishing, count-off, and lights out at about 10:00 p.m. While the squad bay routine didn't change much, there was no serenity in its predictability.

By the end of the first week, the three DIs had gone through their monster patrols often enough for us to feel the strain of the constant ravings. The occasional fist, as well as slaps, started working on the minds of us all. We lived with the knowledge that our present situation was enveloped in a web of fear and uncertainty. That would have to be dealt with if we were to survive the next several months. I suppose we all knew we would not be killed or injured for life, but the constant intimidation exerted by all three DIs started each of us to question how far they would go, and if we were up to the challenge.

We were much like politically repressed prisoners in the intangible feelings and fears that were ever present. Under those threats of violence and abuse, we became progressively smarter in dealing with our environment. The best way to avoid the wrath of the monsters was to do nothing that would draw their attention. I would do everything possible to execute an order or command as quickly and proficiently as I could, all the while trying desperately to remain anonymous. There was safety in not standing out in the crowd. That safety meant security, even if it was only temporary, and even if the ploy was only partially effective. Still, within a platoon of recruits still unsure of themselves and hesitant about their future, that avenue of anonymity worked. At least the monsters appeared to concentrate on the recruits who stood out—either in their inability to perform or in their zest to show their superiority. Attempts to show superiority were almost always crushed by the DIs to keep the continuity of the platoon at a steady pace.

By the end of that second week, I had convinced myself that, no matter what, I was going to leave that Island on the day I was supposed to graduate. No matter the cost. No matter what the monsters did. I was determined to take their orders, their commands and their punishments. I was scared, we all were, but I was even more afraid of the consequences of being set back. So, I adopted the action taken by most of the platoon members. Strive to do what was asked. Excel when possible. Be ready for the punishment. Blend into the background. Live with the fear. Accept the stress. Tolerate the heat. Count the days. It never got easy, and I don't recall I ever really believed it would. But I had never thought that I would live in fear, not before I arrived on the Island.

Competition among the platoons of our series had kept the individual recruits from speaking to one another. We never joined together as a series working together, and were not allowed the privilege of learning any more about the other recruits than they learned about us. It was forbidden to go into another platoon's squad bay or to walk through one of their formations. Walking through a formation was called "breaking ranks," and anyone who committed that offense was immediately attacked by the "offended" platoon.

One dark night after we returned from the rifle range, Ransom Downes and I were sitting on the enclosed stairway landing between the second and third floors enjoying our 2:00 a.m. forbidden cigarette. The firewatch, at our request, had awakened us and we were quietly smoking on the landing above our squad bay, which we determined was more secluded than the one below. An occasional recruit's snore was the only sound that disrupted the quiet of night. It was hot, as usual, and we were clad only in our Marine Corps issue boxer shorts and cotton T-shirt, sitting and enjoying a few relaxed moments.

Sounds of someone's exiting the squad bay on the first floor startled us. We recognized immediately the sound of metal hitting against the steel handrail of the staircase. The Officer of the Day, spot checking to ensure that firewatch rosters were in order, was coming up the stairs! We couldn't go down since the officer would be close enough to see us if we tried to re-enter our own squad bay on the second floor. Going up wasn't attractive to us either since another platoon's squad bay was on that floor, certainly no place for two recruits from 340. In the tense excitement of the moment, I crushed out my cigarette and held my breath, hoping that the officer would enter our own squad bay, giving us time to come up with an alternate plan.

The sound of the officer's climbing the stairs came steadily closer and our fears came true. He was not going inside 340's squad bay. Ransom and I moved at the same instant in the only direction left—up! We were barefooted, so we made no sound on the concrete and steel stairs. As we reached the door of the squad bay upstairs, the sounds of the approaching officer drove us to open the door quietly and slip inside.

This squad bay was identical to our own, but in the darkness it seemed alien. The firewatch must have been back in the classroom area or the showers; in any event, he was nowhere in sight. Our eyes had become accustomed to the darkness and we stopped in fearful silence, trying to decide what to do. We couldn't talk; all we could do to give directions to each other was to push and pull. Quickly, we lay down on two empty bunks closest to the door we had just entered, and froze! I was determined to keep the springs from squeaking at any cost. There had been no time to fold out the mattress so I was lying directly on the springs. I knew that if we were detected by either the firewatch or the officer there was going to be hell to pay when Egge found out. I remember thinking that we would probably be set back as well as beaten, and that our stay on the Island would be extended. I held my breath as the door opened and the officer stepped inside the squad bay.

The firewatch had heard the officer enter and was approaching him. I heard only fragments of their conversation over the pounding of my heart in my ears. The officer asked a few questions and turned to leave. Again, I held my breath as he walked slowly back towards the door. He passed within four feet of the rack I was in but never looked in my direction. As he passed through the door, I almost collapsed from the tension and from holding my breath!

We waited only long enough to ensure that the officer had sufficient time to go downstairs and exit from our barn, then slipped out when the firewatch walked to the opposite end of the bay. We made it without waking anyone and slipped into our friendly bunks. I lay there a long time, my heart pumping like a runaway locomotive, before I fell asleep that night. I almost swore off cigarettes, too.

New games to play and new forms of fear and discipline to master confronted us. One of the favorite new diversions of the monsters was to have us play "watching TV." More often than not, this game was inflicted upon us because someone had made a small slip-up, such as not having his boots in the proper position, or not folding his towel correctly. In order to "watch TV," we were forced to lie on the concrete floor on our stomach, clasp our hands behind our neck (much like you see prisoners do in the movies), then press our elbows downward towards each other while pushing our body up on our toes. In this posture we looked as though we were in the up position of a push-up, only our upper body weight was supported on our elbows, with our hands still clasped behind our neck. The only parts of our body touching the concrete were our elbows and toes. This exercise also may be known as "elbows and toes," but in 340 it was "watching TV."

Not much to the game so far, right? Wrong! The next step is what gave the game its name: We had to sing the theme songs from some of the popular television series and commercials, such as "Winstons taste good, like a cigarette should," and "If you like beer, you'll love Schlitz," and of course, the Mickey Mouse Club theme song. We'd remain in that position until either we dropped or the monster let us up. Although the position is not too difficult to hold for a short period, anything over about two minutes makes the stomach muscles quiver and scream.

To make the game more fun, the monster would patrol up and down the squad bay, pausing to press down gradually on our backs with his boot to exert more weight for us to support, all the while daring us to collapse. I've had Rast put my bucket, full of 782 gear, and my rifle on my back while I was in this position and dare me to let anything fall off. I've stayed in the position long enough to see my reflection in the puddle created from my own sweat underneath me on the painted concrete.

When we finally collapsed, and you can rest assured we would collapse before the monster was through, we would have time only to catch two or three quick breaths before we were forced to reassume the position. The squad bay would fill with grunting and groaning, much like the sounds of weight lifters during their rituals, as we struggled to command all the strength we possessed. It's not a pretty sight, but I lost a few meals while in that position—even collapsed in the mess and had to clean the floor and myself up after we finished the game.

Another of the games consisted of our holding our rifles in front of us, our arms fully extended while we repeated the manual of arms, the chain of command, or even some rule we had broken. This, too, is not difficult at first, as the M-14 weighs only about eight or nine pounds. But after about five minutes of this, the weight of the rifle seems to triple and the stomach and arms start quivering and cramping. It took all our will power and strength to keep our arms extended, and we'd let our arms be cut off rather than drop the rifle on the concrete. Thomson loved this game, and he would patrol up and down the center aisle, sometimes hanging our bucket with 782 gear over the rifle to give us more weight to hold up.

Thomson hung my bucket on my rifle one hot afternoon, then walked up and down the squad bay ranting and raving about how lazy we were. I could no longer hold up the weight of the rifle and bucket, and my arms began slowly moving toward the floor. I eased my arms down just long enough to inhale deeply and was pulling them back to the up position when Thomson saw me and began chewing me out.

My arms were fully extended again, holding the rifle and bucket in their proper position, when he roared in my ear, "What's the matter, Sweetheart? You can't keep up? You gotta problem?"

"No, Sir!" I called back.

He stayed right by my ear and shouted, "You'd best snap outta your shit and get with the program!"

"Yes, Sir!" I answered.

I suppose it either wasn't loud enough or didn't meet with his approval; he hit me with his open palm full on the side of my face, his fingers striking over my ear. It stunned me, but more than that, my ear rang for the rest of the day. I tried to quiet the monster by standing rigid, holding my position and giving no indication that anything had happened. It appeared to work. Thomson growled as he started to walk away, "That's better! You'd best keep me happy!"

My reply was loud and strong, "Yes, Sir!"

I could retire today if I had been paid by the push-up or by the bend-and-thrust exercise, even at the rate of a dollar for each. Both of those exercises were forced upon us as punishment at any hour and for any infraction of the rules. They were exhausting, too, at first, but as time went on and we got in better physical condition, they became easier and were used more sparingly as a form of discipline. The DIs seemed more inclined then to resort to "watching TV" as a group punishment for infractions. Yet other disciplinary methods were indicated by the DIs as they saw fit.

For instance, . . . We had been away from the barn, either at classes or some other training session, and returned to find the entire squad bay in shambles. Bunks had been stripped of their blankets, sheets and pillow cases and thrown haphazardly into piles in the center aisle. Bunks had been turned over and pushed around as though a violent tornado had struck the room. Contents of unlocked locker boxes were spread over the entire squad bay. Mattresses were piled high in the center aisle or simply thrown aside.

As I recall, Corporal Rast was on duty that day, and he arrived before our other DI, Corporal Thomson, had brought us "home." At first I thought some other platoon had sabotaged our squad bay. Then, as we filed in and stood at attention, as close as we could get to standing in what appeared to be the proper place, Corporal Rast roared out with his monster voice, "Miss Downes, get up here!"

A voice answered in reply, "Yes Sir!"

Downes ran over and around the mess and snapped to attention in front of Rast, yelling out, "Private Downes reporting as ordered, Sir!"

"You recognize this?" Rast screamed.

Downes peered down at a cookie Rast was holding out for identification, then replied, "Yes, Sir!"

The rest of us stole glances toward the front to see what was happening. Downes had taken the cookie from the mess hall, brought it back to the squad bay and hidden it in his pillow case, intending to eat it later that night after taps. Rast had spied it during his inspection while we were gone and planned his course of action. He was determined that the entire platoon should learn from example as the discipline was handed out.

We were all commanded to gather around the DI's table up front, which we quickly obeyed, and were permitted to sit down to watch. Rast produced one cookie after another (when he had gone to get them I don't know), thoroughly doused each with Tabasco sauce and instructed Ransom to eat every one. Downes started slowly, his eyes glassy from the Tabasco, but he continued eating until he had consumed about a dozen of the peppery hot cookies. His face turned a few shades of green as he tried in vain to follow Rast's orders to eat them all. Rast continued to harass Downes about "repeat offenses" and "eating in the barn" until Downes at last threw-up. Rast simply smiled, turned and roared out to the rest of us to get the barn squared away (cleaned up). I don't know for a fact, but I doubt if Ransom Downes ever ate another cookie, even without Tabasco sauce.

Ransom was also the "house mouse" for awhile in 340. The house mouse had the dubious distinction of having to take care of the DI's house—cleaning, making up the bunk, bringing iced water, and in general, catering to any whims of the DIs. One day I heard the monster grab Egge and completely take possession as he screamed loudly, "House Mouse, get in here!" Ransom either had not done something right, or had really done something wrong.

At a full run, Ransom yelled, "Yes, Sir!"

When Ransom reached the door he screeched to a halt. The correct procedure was to knock loud and hard until the DI inside replied, "Square the hatch!" At that command, you were to take one step to dead center of the door, face the entrance and report in a loud voice, "Sir, Private _____, reporting as ordered, Sir!"

Ransom was about to knock on the door framing as Rast came out of the DI's house, leaving Egge and Thomson inside. Rast scowled at Downes, "What do you want, Maggot?"

Ransom was not hesitant in replying, "Sir, Sergeant Egge . . ."

Rast's huge hand shot out and grabbed Downes' throat in a choke hold as he roared, "Who?"

Ransom struggled to respond even louder, though obviously in pain, "Sir, Sergeant Egge . . . the Drill Instructor!"

Several fists in the stomach followed, with Rast repeatedly yelling the same question. Ransom looked confused as well as hurt as Rast continued the beating. Each time Ransom replied "Sir, Sergeant Egge," Rast would hit him again. Rast was furious and the monster had full control. Just as I thought Ransom would be knocked unconscious, Thomson stepped out of the DI's house. As Ransom responded to Rast's question for about the sixth time, again obviously incorrectly, Thomson interceded by screaming at Ransom, "Do you mean your Senior Drill Instructor?"

Ransom had the presence of mind to reply quickly, "Sir, yes, Sir! My Senior Drill Instructor, Sir!"

Rast then shoved Ransom away, and in a disgusted sneer demanded, "Get the fuck outta my sight!"

Ransom yelled "Yes, Sir!" and returned to his rack, bruised and hurting from his beating. Rast had beaten him for not replying "Sir, my Senior Drill Instructor" instead of "Sergeant Egge." For that small error, Ransom had received his 340 discipline. Ransom never found out what Egge had summoned him for, as Egge never came out of his quarters during the entire encounter.

That beating brings to my mind another beating Ransom received from Rast. I don't remember the infraction, but Ransom was at his rack when Rast started in on him. The monster quickly took charge and Ransom was again grabbed in a choke hold by Rast. He proceeded to choke Ransom, slamming him against the steel frame of the bunk and punching him in the midsection with his fists. Ransom was left lying in the floor as Rast walked up the center aisle acting as though nothing had happened.

When a recruit was under siege by one of the DIs, all of the other recruits, though sympathetic, gave no appearances of witnessing the drama. After all, it could easily have been any one of us. When the monster was loose, the safest approach for the rest of us was, again, to blend in to avoid drawing their attention. We would act as though we had heard and seen nothing and pretend to be totally engrossed in some other chore, head and eyes purposely in any direction except that of the recipient of the monster's actions. I sometimes wonder if Downes, now in business with his father in Orlando, ever utilizes the benefits of those hot days of discipline.

Another nightly ritual we performed, either just before or immediately after counting off, was the recitation of one of several things we were required to commit to memory. At first, we were allowed to read these out loud from our notes. Some of them were simply learned by rote.

One of the things 340 had to recite was the chain of command. We would start at the top of the chain, loudly, "Sir, the President of the United States is John F. Kennedy." We would not go through the remaining political chain of command but jump to the Marine Corps chain with "Sir, the Commandant of the Marine Corps is General David M. Shoup." Then we would recite the name of the Commander of the Recruit Training Depot of Parris Island, the Commander of the Third Recruit Training Battalion, the Company Commander, the Company Senior Noncommissioned Officer, and Series Commander, the Series Gunnery Sergeant and then the Drill Instructors.

On other nights we would recite our General Orders, a list of "dos and don'ts" for every sentry on guard duty. These instructions are universal in the military and are intended to protect life and property. Again, we read them aloud in unison until we could recite them from memory, which did not take long. There are eleven General Orders, and they were recited to the DIs in the same fashion as the chain of command. Standing rigidly at the position of attention, we would yell, "Sir, my first General Order is to take charge of this post and all government property in view!" I'll not challenge my memory to recall all eleven of the General Orders, but the last one was, "Sir, the eleventh General Order is to be especially watchful at night and during the time for challenging, and to challenge all persons on or near my post, and to allow no one to pass without proper authority!" How's that, Egge? And after almost twenty years!

After the DIs had sent us to bed, but before the lights were turned off, we would often recite the words of "The Marines Hymn." We were not allowed to sing the song because, according to Egge, "That ain't your song until the band plays it when you graduate." That seemed fair, but there were times when each recruit feared he would never hear that band.

Another phase of squad bay life was "clean and press," which took place each weekend. Simply put, that was our wash day, executed outside between the barracks on long, waist-high concrete tables which had faucets running along the full length, about fourteen or sixteen inches above the table top. We carried our dirty clothes there in our buckets, along with a bottle of Wisk in the familiar red plastic dispenser, and did our laundry (sans washer and dryer technology), hung it on the clothesline and returned later to gather it in.

As usual, the gag order allowing no talking was enforced, although a whisper to the nearest recruit would sometimes go unheard by the DI. On this day, Steve Willard, from Winston Salem, North Carolina, was the violator of the gag rule. I'm not sure which instructor was on duty at the time, but I remember the consequences all too vividly. The enraged DI screamed and cursed Willard and backed him against the concrete wash rack, yelling in his face. I don't recall whether Willard was hit by the DI, but before the next fifteen minutes were over, I think Willard, had he been given a choice, would gladly have taken the fist in the stomach over what the DI had in store.

The monster made Willard pour a good stiff squirt of the liquid Wisk into a warm canteen of water, then drink it until, like Downes, he threw up. It wasn't pretty, but you can bet it was effective. It may seem strange to some people who read this, but following instructions like drinking warm, soapy water was much easier than the consequences of disobeying an order. At least you could do it quickly and be done with it rather than suffer a physical beating, an act which by now had been witnessed by all of 340. And we were sure that we had not seen the limits of severity in those physical "encounters."

I recall another time, one night, when the gag rule was broken. Rast was on duty, and my side of the squad bay was showering and shaving. I had just completed both and returned to my rack, sat down and started cleaning some of my gear. Rast jumped to his feet from his chair at the DI's table and yelled out, "Who the hell is talking in the shower?"

There was no reply. In typical fashion, Rast went into a rage, yelling and screaming that we knew we weren't supposed to talk unless directed by our DIs. He went on and on. Finally, he made everyone on our side of the barracks strip down, take our soap and re-enter the shower. Now, the shower room was only about twelve feet by twelve feet, and thirty-five of us had to get in that tiny room together. We were packed in tightly as Rast stood at the door, fidgeting to start playing one of his games. "You want to talk in my shower?" he yelled. To which we replied "No, Sir!" Of course, the reply wasn't loud enough, so he made us turn on the cold water. Normally, a cool shower was exhilarating on the hot summer nights, but with only the cold water it was freezing.

Rast yelled again, "You think you can be quiet now, Ladies?"

"Yes, Sir!" we responded.

His reply still indicated rage, "That ain't gonna get it, Ladies! Turn off the cold water and turn on the hot!" The water temperature changed quickly, and steam filled the room as we stood in the spray of the hot water. There was no way to move since we were packed in so tightly; all we could do was stand there. Rast kept this up for awhile, then told us to lie down on the floor. Lie down? We could barely all stand in the shower and there was no way to lie down, but we tried. "Now, do you think you can keep your fucking mouths shut in my shower?" he roared.

The barn may have shaken with our reply, "Yes, Sir!"

Even that didn't suit Rast. He gave us a new directive, "Stand up!" We had all struggled back to an upright position when he continued, "Hold your soap over your head in your right hand!" When he saw that we all had complied, he continued, "Now drop it!" When there were only empty hands in the air, he gave us a sickening order to follow, which we did. I'll not go into details, but I'll tell you that his next command was uttered in a low and disgusting tone as he said, "Now, . . . pick it up!" You form your own pictures of our complying to that order.

After a short while, Rast sent us to our racks. The game was over, thank God. I never found out who had talked in the shower that night. For his health and safety, it was better that way. We never played that game again. But then, there was no way you could have persuaded 340 to talk in the shower again.

The DIs were always ready with different and varied forms of "fun and games" to make their point. On one particular Saturday, someone left a towel in the shower after a rainy morning P.T. session and the DI found it. He came raging into the squad bay, yelling, "You ladies can't keep up with your gear?" Without waiting for an answer, he continued, "You ain't pleased with the Corps? O.K., damnit, when you get tired of where you are, you move, and that's what we'll do!" We didn't know it, but we were preparing to play "moving house."

The DI stormed up and down the center aisle. "Close the fucking windows and fall in at your racks!" he screamed. There was a mad rush to close the windows, and we were all rigidly at attention when he continued, "Pick up your locker box on your left shoulder!" We obeyed even though it was awkward and heavy. "When I give the command," he continued, "you will face to the right and march up one side of the center aisle, square the corners, and continue down the other side of the aisle. As you reach the table on this end, you'll square the corners and complete the rectangle. You'll do this until I tell you what else to do!"

We had no idea what was to follow, but at this command we started marching single file in the rectangle formed by the center aisle, all the while carrying our locker boxes. The DI stood on the table at one end of the squad bay and barked his commands and cadence so we could keep in step. Our questions didn't have to wait long for an answer as he loudly commanded, "Platoon . . . Halt!" We froze and, after a brief pause, he continued, "Take your right hand, reach in your locker box and pull out your left shower shoe!" He waited until each of us had the shower shoe in his hand. Satisfied that we had the correct item, he shouted, "Throw it over your left shoulder into the center aisle!" After that was completed, he commanded, "Forward ... March!" We started marching again in rectangular fashion as we had before. We had gone about twenty steps when his next command roared out, "Platoon . . . Halt! Now reach in your locker box and take out a pair of socks and throw them over your left shoulder!"

This process was repeated over and over until we had emptied our locker boxes of all our clothing, extra uniforms, belts and most of our personal gear, including our shaving kits. When I looked at the rectangle bordered by all the recruits, there was a huge mound of mixed up items all heaped together, distinguished only by our ink-stamped names on each item. But there was no way to know who had thrown which item where. The real "fun" was still ahead.

The DI marched us around until we were back at our own racks. The heat had become almost unbearable with the windows closed. As we resumed the position of attention, he waited, saying nothing for a short time, then looked at his watch and roared, "All right, Ladies, you got five minutes to find your gear, store it properly and be ready for an inspection! Ready . . . Go!"

If there ever was anything that represented what is called a Chinese fire drill, we were it. There was a scramble for gear that turned to outright mayhem as each man looked for his personal belongings. I found my shaving kit, a shower shoe, one belt and a pair of utility trousers. I returned those to my locker box and started to search for the remaining items when he boomed out, "O.K., Ladies, time's up!" We quickly returned to the position of attention at our racks, aware that the mound had lowered only slightly.

He was seething. "What the fuck's the problem, Ladies?" he screamed, "You think I'm playing when I tell you to get your shit together?"

We were all tired and drenched in sweat, but we managed to approximate enthusiasm as we yelled loudly, "No, Sir!"

"O.K.," he yelled, "then we'll try it again! Pick up your locker boxes!"

We went through the rectangular marching routine and, again, upon his command, emptied what few items we had retrieved in the initial scramble. Our being in constant motion, the heat had gotten worse, and our enthusiasm had been dealt a blow since we now knew we would have to repeat the retrieval process. He was not through, yet, though, and had another surprise as we fell back in at the foot of our racks.

The DI casually surveyed the mess again, then commanded, "This time, Ladies, you're going to have to show me how bad you want your own gear! I want to hear you get mean! I want you to show me how fast you can move your asses! This time you got *three* minutes!" He paused, looked us over, and summed it up for us. "You Ladies have got to fight for what's yours! If somebody's got your gear, I want to see you take it back! Ready . . . Go!''

Needless to say, we didn't accomplish the feat in our scheduled three minutes. If we couldn't do it in five, we all knew we couldn't do it in three, but we tried. He had us repeat the exercise twice more, with the last attempt to be one minute. By that time, tempers were short; the heat only added to our frustration. Half of us were fighting among ourselves, and the other half were trying to comply with his demands. We were exhausted from the chaotic game when he finally called an end to it. ''You fucking Maggots make me sick!'' he roared. ''Clean up this mess!'' He sat back in his chair, propped his feet up on the table, and sat quietly as we worked for an hour or more to restore order to the squad bay and our foot lockers. We would play that game again before the summer was over.

''Summertime, and the living is easy . . . .''

VIII

WEEKENDS

VIII

W EEKENDS ON THE ISLAND were much the same as other days except for two things. First, all classes were given by the DIs since the regular teachers had weekends off; and second, there was church. Religion had its place in our training but it was treated much like any other class. Members of the Jewish faith as well as Protestants and Catholics had services on Sunday. I fell in with my fellow Protestant recruits, was marched over to the small chapel by a DI, ordered inside and told to sit. We would sing a song, listen to a short sermon by the chaplain, sing another song and it was over. I resented that the Marine Corps had invaded even my religion, as they carried the Marine Corps flag, the U.S. flag and the Christian flag down the aisle before and at the close of the service. The DI was present the whole time, and from all outward appearances was there to see that we did no talking and followed orders. Somehow it never seemed right to have to sit at the position of attention during church. It did seem appropriate under those conditions that the first song we sang was "Onward Christian Soldiers."

One Sunday after we had returned from the rifle range, one of the Jewish recruits informed me that they enjoyed some of the luxuries we all dreamed about. Specifically, he explained that the rabbi would give them a short message, go through the traditional Jewish ceremony and then allow all the recruits about thirty minutes to write letters, drink Cokes and smoke cigarettes prior to releasing them to return to their barracks. Such liberties were unbelievable to me, especially since our Protestant services were so rigidly watched over by the DIs. I decided that I wanted to look further into this!

That weekend Egge called out his customary command, "Jewish—take one step forward!" With only a short hesitation, I, too, stepped out. "Moore, what the hell are you doing?" Egge boomed.

Trying to sound more convincing than I felt, I sang out, "Sir, I'm converting!" Egge looked at me as though he wasn't sure if I was serious or crazy. I, along with the Jewish recruits, waited as Egge stood for a second before ordering, "Get outside!"

Thomson marched us over to the synagogue, leaving as we entered. To understand my feelings upon entering the synagogue, maybe I ought to tell you that I had been raised a Southern Baptist, and I felt, to say the least, awkward. I knew nothing of Jewish theology or customs, so I had to watch my fellow recruits as we entered in order to follow their lead. Even now, I'm embarrassed to say I don't know if the little bowl-like caps have a special name, but the recruits, including myself, donned their caps and the service began. If there was ever any time when the saying "I felt like a whore in Sunday school" was appropriate, it applied to me during that Jewish service! I had had no exposure to the Hebrew language, and—you guessed it— the whole service was in Hebrew. I had no idea what the chants said or meant. The only time I knew what was going on was when they bowed their heads in prayer, and even then I couldn't tell what they were praying about. I fervently joined in silent prayer. I prayed that Goldberg hadn't lied about the Cokes, letters and cigarettes.

After another short message in Hebrew, there was another chant and the service was over. Anxious to see what would happen next, I hung back, not wanting to be the first to enter the adjoining room. I followed Goldberg through the door opening into an air-conditioned room. My prayer had been answered: I saw a couple of packs of Winston cigarettes and two packs of Salems; real honest-to-God, ice-cold Cokes were heaped on the tables, as well as a good supply of writing paper and pens. The next half-hour was a glorious relief from the fear and stress-packed life of the Island. I filled my stomach with Coke, my lungs with smoke, my skin with air conditioning, and friends and loved ones with letters! We returned to the barracks, and I didn't pass along the secret of the activities at the synagogue until after we graduated. The following week when time for religious services approached, Egge stayed "one up" on me as he proclaimed, "All the Jews and Moore get outside!"

I've never been able to convince myself that the DIs were unaware of the activities of the Jewish recruits in the synagogue. Surely, someone had to have let the word out!

We were back to the regular grind on Monday after church services. Egge, Rast and Thomson rotated their schedules so that we could enjoy their smiling faces, two at a time during the day and one of them all night. We could breathe a little easier when Thomson had night duty. He was less inclined to get into any "heavy" discipline as long as we did what was expected. He would hit us if we screwed up, but his punches were, shall I say, "less severe" than those of his counterparts, and he would demand perhaps fifty push-ups instead of seventy-five.

Thomson when on night duty would usually allow us reasonable time to write letters home. Egge and Rast always had us cleaning equipment and playing games so that it was not unusual to have only a minute or less to write. I still have the letters I wrote home, and there are several of only one page which took two and sometimes three nights to write merely because the DI had us cleaning and polishing until "lights out." Several times I stayed awake and slipped into the head to complete a letter after the DI was asleep. Those times were rare, though, as sleep was always in short supply and letters seemed to matter less than the much-needed rest. Still, they were our only contact with the outside world, and we waited like hungry animals for mail call each night, starved for word from loved ones and information about local, state and national news which we were unable to receive otherwise.

We had been informed early in our training that the Marine Corps welcomed guests while we were in training so long as the visit occurred on Sunday afternoon and didn't take up too much of our time. That turned into a big joke quickly, a bad joke at that. The DIs told us that we had best not discourage visitors, but that it would not please them if 340 had "guests." The reason was simple enough, according to them. First, there were those of us from a long way off, such as New York and Wisconsin, whose families could not afford the expense of traveling that distance for a short visit, so it would be unfair to them if those of us who lived closer took advantage of guest privileges. Second, it would "affect" our attitude towards our training. It would not allow us to keep the proper mental approach to our basic training, and therefore, would "probably" cause us to lose ground and "maybe" even set us back in the graduation schedule.

Since I lived only seventy-five miles from the Island, guests, family and fiancée were sure to make the trip unless I specifically told them not to come, which was impossible since we had been told to inform them that guests were welcome. I suffered the worst beating after my fiancée, Kathy, and parents showed up about our sixth Sunday on the Island. Rast was on duty that day and we were cleaning rifles when a company runner came in, walked over and whispered something into Rast's ear. With a cold look of contempt and hatred in his voice, he bellowed, "Moore, get up here!"

I scrambled to my feet, ran behind the bunks and up to the DI's table and replied, "Sir, Private Moore, reporting as ordered, Sir!"

His disgust now even more apparent, he growled, "You got guests! You see me when you get home, Sweetheart! Go get on your utility (combat) shirt and report to Company HQ."

"Sir, yes, Sir!" I replied as I turned around and rushed to do as Rast had ordered. I knew when he told me "see me when you get home, Sweetheart" that a beating would ensue. That statement had been made to us many times before when we were in view of too many "eyes" for the DIs to inflict 340 discipline at the time of a particular infraction. It served to put us on warning that we had screwed up and punishment would take place when we got back to the barn. Maybe worrying about it only made it seem worse, but it seemed as though the DIs put more of themselves into the execution of postponed punishment than into punishment given impromptu at the time of the violation.

I spent a short hour or two with my parents and Kathy, fully appreciative of the time we had but aware of what was awaiting me. I was not disappointed; that is, the reception Rast had promised did live up to my anticipation.

When I returned to the squad bay, I reported to the DI's house as Rast had ordered. Going past the door, I did an about-face and went through the mandatory procedure of reporting, furiously knocking on the wall beside the door. Rast's voice from inside snarled out, "What do you want?"

I yelled back, "Sir, Private Moore reporting as ordered!"

The tone of his reply held the same contempt as before. "Square the hatch!" he growled.

I took one step towards the center of the door, faced smartly to the left, and stood facing the open door. Rast sat casually at the desk, leaning back in the chair with his feet propped up and ankles crossed. By this time in our training, I knew the correct position of attention and procedure for reporting. As I stood there I mentally went over each phase of the rules to ensure I was doing nothing to arouse the beast in Rast. Deep down I knew it would make no difference, but I figured it wouldn't hurt if I presented my best efforts. Rast dropped his feet to the floor, put his pen on the desk, stood up and took the three or four steps toward me that would put us only inches apart.

In a menacing and cocky, though lowered, voice he queried, "Well, Sweetheart, how were your guests?"

Fairly certain of what was to follow, I answered, "The family is fine, Sir!"

"Well," he continued in his sneering voice, "while you were gone I happened to be by your rack and found some rust on the front sight of your rifle. Rust means it wasn't cleaned properly! If you had been thinking about that instead of having guests, that would never have happened, now would it?"

"No, Sir!" I replied.

His next move didn't come as a surprise either, but the shock stifled any further ability to respond as he grabbed me by the neck with his huge left hand. I had seen him do this before to fellow recruits. He put his thumb on one side of my neck and his fingers on the other, then squeezed tightly and lifted up, all the while pushing in on my Adam's apple with his knuckle and making it impossible to speak. Rast was big and strong, so his upward pressure on my neck brought me up on my toes. In rag-doll fashion, he pushed me across the small corridor outside the DI's house, still lifting up and shoving me back as I tried to stay on my feet. He then slammed me against the concrete block wall, not once but three or four times, while increasing his pressure on my neck and cutting off the blood circulation to my head. He continued to put pressure on my Adam's apple and question me, knowing that I couldn't answer.

With his right hand, he now slapped me across the face for not answering his first question. By now, the beast had full control; the best I could hope for was that it wouldn't last too long. I suppose he could tell by the color in my face when to ease off on my neck, and as he relaxed his grip on my throat ever so slightly, he countered with a right fist to my stomach. His eyes flashed fury mixed with love of power as he continued unchecked his barrage of questions. A back hand slap drew the taste of blood in my mouth and he again slapped me with his broad palm. The pressure on my neck was increased again and I was choking. Another fist in the stomach made me feel the urge to throw up, but his tight grip on my throat made it impossible even if I had tried. Several more slaps and fists to the stomach and Rast released me. I tried to remain standing but it was no use. My legs simply wouldn't lock in place and I slid down the wall to a half-sitting, half-squatting position on the floor.

"Next time, Sweetheart," Rast snarled quietly in my face as he leaned down and snapped my face up to his, "you'd best remember that your gear is more important than your guests!"

The entire platoon had its "oblivious to everything" face on but had listened to and seen at least a part of the entire session. The message was loud and clear—guests lead to trouble.

Each recruit with visitors had some 340 discipline to face after his guests had left. The DIs would always do as Rast had and find something to make it appear as though the guests weren't the cause of the discipline. I suppose that could be an "out" for them if there were repercussions from "higher-ups." The difficult part of the problem was to discourage guests when the official Marine Corps position was to encourage them, and the burden of doing both was left to the recruit.

Weekends, we usually would have a "field day." If that sounds like fun, don't run down to your Marine Corps Recruiter just yet. A field day is when we cleaned the squad bay from ceiling to concrete floor, everything from the toilets to the springs on the bunks. Generally, we'd have to do it all over again. Windows sparkled, as did painted surfaces scrubbed with stiff-bristled brushes and soap and water, then rinsed. Even the stairs were scrubbed, sometimes with toothbrushes. Even that sometimes had to be done over. The heat of the Island summer only made those field days longer and harder.

One of the treasured jobs during field day was the job of cleaning the stairs outside the squad bay. We filled our buckets from the outside faucets to rinse off the staircase. If we were careful, we could sneak a drink of cool water from the bucket after getting back in the closed confines of the staircase. If we drank from the faucet we ran the risk of being seen by the DI through the upstairs windows. And the beast!

IX

CLASSES

NUMEROUS HOURS WERE SPENT in the classroom studying every subject that the new recruits needed to complete the
transformation from civilian to Marine. In the Third Battalion,
most of those classes were held in one of the single-story brick
buildings across the grinder behind our barracks. Most of the
classrooms were furnished with chairs and tables, so we could
place an item of equipment on the table for inspection or for a
step-by-step practical application in assembly and maintenance,
such as the classes on the .45 caliber pistol. Most classrooms also
had blackboards and visual training aids, such as a two-foot by
four-foot tablet mounted on a tripod, whose pages could be
lifted up and folded over to expose another page of facts we
were to learn. Even though rooms might be air-conditioned, it
was kept off and the windows—the roll-out type—were opened.

Some of the classes were for a platoon-size group and others
could house two platoons. I remember only two classrooms

large enough to hold the entire series, and they were used when we had a class involving only a lecture format. Lectures were given on topics such as the History of the Marine Corps and the Uniform Code of Military Justice. There seemed to be more time spent in the classroom during the first several weeks of training than later.

The one common denominator among the classrooms was the heat. Even with the windows full open, there was the omnipresent hot summer temperatures, hovering forever it seemed near the 100-degree mark. It was extremely difficult to maintain a long attention span under the lazy heat in those classrooms, especially at classes immediately after lunch. That was the worst time, since nighttime sleep was scarce and stomachs were full. I can remember trying with all my ability to pay attention to a lecturer, only to feel the eyelids of lead start to close. The voice of the teacher would slip out into a distant haze, then return as I realized I was about to doze off. With a start I opened my eyes wide. The DIs patrolled the class looking for anyone dozing or not paying attention. When the lectures were boring, the classes long and the temptation to doze too much to overcome, I've seen the DIs walk up behind a recruit whose head slowly dropped to the chin-resting-on-chest position and sharply slap him on the back of the neck to jolt him back to the sitting position of attention.

Of course we played the seats game upon our arrival at these classes, and we had come to anticipate the sameness of that ritual. Some of the history classes dealt with famous names of past heroes of the Corps. Names like Puller, famous for his aggressive leadership, and Lejeune, who would later have a Marine Corps base named for him. We were taught the dates of famous Marine Corps victories and battles of past wars. Those classes were looked upon by most recruits as brief rest from the physically demanding schedule of the outdoor exercise and training.

We were issued a small spiral notebook in which to jot down

class notes we would need to refer to in later phases of training. They were small, about two by five inches, the spiral at the top. They fit handily in our hip pockets, and we carried those notebooks practically everywhere we went while in boot camp. During classes, I found that the most effective method of staying awake was to take notes. Sometimes I gravitated to the art world and scribbled stick figures during especially boring lectures. We also did crude drawings of the parts of some of the weapons and studied these periodically.

Those study times were scheduled for "any time you are not doing something else I have instructed you to do," as Egge put it. One of the sights of Parris Island I'll always remember is that of a recruit who, after finishing eating, had run outside to stand in platoon formation at the position of attention. Reaching into his pocket and pulling out his notebook, the recruit would hold it up to his face and study until the remainder of the platoon joined the ranks and the DI instructed us to put away our study aids.

I was standing outside the mess hall after the noontime meal one early July day, studying my notes while waiting for the rest of 340 to finish eating. I had been reviewing my notes from a lecture on the Uniform Code of Military Justice. I turned the page and found that the next page was filled with my stick-figure art forms. I wasn't really in a mood to study, and I started daydreaming with the notebook held in front of my face. From a distance anyone would have assumed I was engrossed in my notes, practicing the good study habits of a Marine recruit. The sun was high and hot as I stood on the grinder, totally immersed in faraway thoughts. Only four or five other recruits were outside with me, and they, too, were standing with notebooks in front of their noses, apparently studying.

Egge and Thomson had been with us that morning, and neither had emerged from the mess hall yet. Rast would soon be on duty, but since a recruit was not allowed a watch, one could only guess at the time. I was so engrossed in my daydream that I was totally startled by the low snarl of Rast close to my ear: "Outstanding, Miss Moore! Out-fucking-standing! What are you? Some kind of fucking artist?"

He had absolutely scared the hell out of me. I had been so deep in thought that I hadn't had the slightest warning of his advance. Evidently, he had come on duty and, not having found us at the barn, had known he would find us at the mess hall. He had slipped up behind me, looked over my shoulder and found me apparently studying my stick figures! I quickly answered, "Sir, no, Sir!"

"Well, Sweetheart, which class did those notes come from?" he queried.

"Sir," I replied, "I drew them in the squad bay!" That was the only reply I could come up with at the time.

"Well, you see me when we get home, Sweetheart!"

I knew what that meant. The wait outside the mess hall was not a long one and we turned towards the barn. My thoughts were centered around the forthcoming encounter with Rast, and I recall thinking that there was just no end to the whole damn cycle. Back to the barn. Report to the DI's house. Screaming by Rast. Choke hold and two slaps. Back to my rack. Egge's yelling, "Chrome domes, cartridge belts and rifles . . . Stand by to fall out for drill!" Back outside. Hot sun. Sweat. Drill. More Sweat. It never ended.

Some of our classes, such as hand-to-hand combat, were given outdoors in the glaring sun of mid-afternoon, but during a few we were permitted to sit on bleachers in the shade of large live oak trees. That shade was a welcomed relief to us even if it would last only thirty minutes. Still, the outdoor class presented less opportunity for the mind to wander, for most of them led to some physical aspect of our training and we would have to practice and implement our lessons immediately after the class.

There were two disadvantages to the outdoor classes. First, there was the ever-present and sweltering heat. While it was manifest during almost every phase and location of our training, it seemed to burn right through our clothing as we sat in the sun listening to lectures. The second was Parris Island's famous parasite: the sand flea, a very small creature which lives in sandy regions and whose single purpose on Parris Island appeared to be the total annihilation of the population by injecting venom around the ears, eyes, nose and neck of its victims. A bite by one of these tiny creatures is like the prick of a red-hot needle penetrating the skin. The almost immediate result is a broad red whelp. The tiny-but-sharp bite immediately draws an almost involuntary slap, followed by a persistent urge to scratch to soothe the pain.

That slap or scratch, though, invariably brought the recruit into conflict with one of the rules of the DIs. "If they don't eat, you don't eat," meaning the recruit would have to miss his next meal. It also led the DI's adding one of his standard 340 dictates for that violation—"You see me when we get home, Sweetheart." The sand flea attacks at all hours, day or night, and is especially addicted to recruits. It is even fonder of recruits who are new on the island. Mosquitoes have a reputation for severe bites, but they can't even hold the door for the sand flea. Time after time while we were standing in formation outside the mess hall, the sand flea would attack as we stood rigidly at attention.

It took time, but slowly, one bite at a time, we became accustomed to the savage attacks of both the mosquito and the sand flea. I can't fully understand it now, but after a few short weeks we were able to ignore the bites of these pests. The pain of the bite was blocked out mentally, likely by the fear of the greater pain that a DI would inject if we responded to the bite. I got to the point where I could watch a mosquito alight on my arm, stick his small stinger into the skin and suck away the blood, yet I felt no pain at all.

Bayonet training classes were taught on the grinder across the road behind the mess hall. Each offensive and defensive maneuver was shown step-by-step by another of the endless string of Marine Corps instructors. The maneuvers were then practiced by us. First, we would walk through each maneuver, then speed up the motion until it became a ballet movement for combat. After several classes on the basics, we moved over to a bayonet course out beyond the grinder.

This course is made up of five poles spaced approximately ten yards apart. A cross member at the top of each pole extends some six feet on either side of it. Suspended by a rope from this cross member is a cylindrical heavy canvas bag shaped like those on which boxers practice punching. Likewise, it is stuffed to make it rigid. Another rope attached to the bottom anchors the bag to a steel eye-ring embedded in the ground. The ropes are pulled tight so the bag remains relatively still, but it has the capacity to spin if a bayonet thrust hits the bag off center. We ran from one post to the next, hitting each bag with a particular thrust or slash. About the third time it would cease to be fun, and the sweat-drenched bodies continued the drill on sheer determination.

Then came the pugil sticks, which were nothing more than four-foot-long sticks with padding at each end. Two men faced each other in a circle about six feet in diameter, each man wearing a football helmet with a face mask and a groin protector. The object of the game was to knock the opponent down, using either padded end of the stick, and it was used as a tool to teach a recruit to be aggressive. Those battles quickly turned into brawls, the DIs always yelling and screaming for combatants to get more aggressive. Each time there was a knock-down, the DIs would enthusiastically encourage the winner and scowl at the man on the ground. The rougher the fight, the happier the DIs and instructors were.

After several sessions, a competition to find the best pugil stick fighter in the Series ensued. We started the elimination process in two circles, with the winners of each contest waiting to pair off. The fights were fierce, and even with the protective devices, there were a few bloody noses and split lips. The fighting finally narrowed to the two surviving recruits in our platoon, and I can remember only that I wasn't one of them. I had lost in my third fight against a recruit from Orlando, Florida, Jimmy Kidwell. The winner was then matched against the other platoon winners of our Series for the grand finale. Platoon 342 won that, so Egge wasn't too pleased. At least it was early in the training schedule and we would have other chances to redeem ourselves.

Each Marine recruit is given courses and tests in swimming. If a recruit passes the basic swimming tests, he advances to the combat swimming lessons where he is taught how to swim with his combat gear, including packs. If he fails his initial swimming test, he is given elementary classes to teach him to swim. Fear of the water must be overcome if one has such a fear. We learned that determination can overcome what may seem an insurmountable problem.

Take Palmer, a small black recruit who always gave his all. On the morning of our swim tests, Palmer hit the water like all the rest of us, but he came up sputtering and spitting, gasping for air. It was obvious that he couldn't make it. Egge, standing by the edge of the pool and seeing Palmer struggling, yelled out at him, "Palmer! What's the matter?"

As Palmer gasped for another breath of air, he called back, "I can't swim, Sir!"

"Then what the hell are you doing?" screamed Egge.

Palmer's head would go under, then bob back up as he flailed and splashed towards the opposite end of the pool. His half-choked response was full of determination as he called back, "I'll make it, Sir!"

I had just completed my test as Palmer had jumped in and I watched in silence the whole episode. Palmer was close to the side of the pool and Egge leaned forward to observe him closely, walking side-step down the pool's edge and getting wet himself from the frenetic splashing of the recruit. Palmer's determination had ignited a small fire in Egge's eye and the DI was going to see him through. But so was Palmer.

Another ten yards and Palmer appeared to be under the water

more than on top. His sputtering and splashing had aroused the attention of the swimming instructors, one of whom came over and started to dive in and help Palmer.

Egge stopped him with a yell, "No, let him go!"

The instructor looked questioningly at Egge but obeyed his wishes. Egge turned and looked down again at Palmer and hollered, "Palmer, you need help?"

Palmer's reply was again half-choked and sputtering as he answered breathlessly, "I'll make it, Sir!"

That enthusiasm excited Egge as he yelled, "Damn right you'll make it! Keep going!"

By now, Palmer's struggle had caught the attention of everyone there and cheers of encouragement rang out, echoing in the large enclosed building housing the pool. Palmer had passed the halfway point without perfecting any style at all. His arms and legs were splashing and grabbing for each extra inch and foot he could get. Egge by now was down on his hands and toes, crab-walking along the pool's edge, caught up in the excitement.

"Go! Palmer, you can make it!" he encouraged.

Palmer could no longer answer. He had almost completed the hundred-yard swim and was all but totally exhausted. For the final twenty yards, Egge was absolutely beside himself with excitement. Palmer was exhibiting what the Corps was all about; never quit—push forward—succeed when failure is inevitable. Egge continued yelling encouragement, calling Palmer John Paul Jones, after the famous historical figure who refused to give up the ship. As Palmer's hand reached out to grasp the end of the pool, signaling completion of the test, Egge literally jerked Palmer out of the water, and in his enthusiasm hugged him, oblivious to the fact that his uniform was now drenched from contact with the exhausted swimmer. From that day on, the DIs called Palmer by his new name, John Paul Jones.

X

THE GRINDER

ENDLESS HOURS OF PRACTICING on drill maneuvers, rifle handling (Manual of Arms), and sweat, sweat, sweat, were spent on the grinder. In this paved parade area, the DIs would give us close-order drill and then put us through the maneuver over and over until we did it in our sleep at night. These sessions could last a few minutes or for hours. The sun beat down unmercifully on the hot pavement, and the heat would penetrate the very soles of our combat boots.

To teach a platoon all the facing maneuvers as well as the movements of a platoon in motion was no easy task, and I don't envy the DIs that phase of their job. Instructions and examples had to be repeated, rehearsed, repeated and practiced. Each of us slowly proceeded to improve, but not without the constant stare of the observant DIs and not without long, hot hours of sweaty repetition.

Egge seemed especially driven to see us excel in the rudiments of close-order drill. He had time and time again told us that

"The platoon who can master close-order drill is the platoon who has learned to work as a team, and that's what the Corps is all about!" He drove us to damn near exhaustion, repeating and practicing morning, noon and even at night.

If you've never heard a Marine Corps DI count cadence in his inimitable sing-song style, then I'm never going to be able to describe it. I will say that the sounds are more of a feeling than understandable commands, put together in the musical imagination of the individual DI. No two sound exactly alike, but you can take any Marine, put him in a platoon under any DI, and he can execute the commands, even though to the public the sounds are more like jumbled musical notes than commands.

On a scale of one to ten, with ten being the best, I'd have to give Egge a twelve. As he marched us along, he even sang cadence to the tune of "The Marines Hymn." Rest assured, he worked our tails off on the grinder, but when we turned towards the barracks, he would start another song, leading us to, as he would say, "lean back" and "strut." He worked at teaching us the execution, exaggerating I'm sure the importance of being "exact" and "snappy" in each position and with every step. His favorite phrase was "Lean back! Diggem in, and strut, strut, strut!" encouraging us literally to try and dig our heels into the pavement with each step. He worked as hard as we did on the grinder. He had told us repeatedly, "Every time you're in formation, you check and recheck your position and alignment. Whenever I look at 340, all I want to see is four rows of corn, just like on the farm." The other two DIs reflected Egge's demands for excellence in drilling and they all pushed us unendingly to achieve success.

Platoon 340 gained proficiency slowly, but with each small success came the confidence we needed to move on to something more complicated. Platoon 340 appeared to be either more dedicated or simply more accomplished than the other platoons of our series. It wasn't until we had graduated, gone on to more combat training at Camp Lejeune in North Carolina, and met some of the members of those other platoons that we found out they had all been aware of 340's drilling skill. Egge must have known, but he simply wouldn't let up.

Egge, Rast and Thomson kept us on the grinder for special close-order drill, maneuvers much like the complicated and intricate exercises one sees special drill teams from military colleges perform. Those lessons were given to us only if we "earned" them. Later on, we found that the more time we spent on the grinder working on these special drills, the less time we spent in the barn playing games.

Sometimes the sun on the grinder would be so hot that shimmering heat ripples from the pavement were visible as we looked over towards the command buildings or the mess hall. Sweat was the cheapest commodity on the Island, but it belonged to the recruits, not the seasoned veterans stationed there. Hands became so sweaty it was difficult to hold a rifle properly on our shoulders as we marched. Rivulets of sweat trickled down our faces, necks and arms. It flowed into our eyes, burning slightly, and reminding us of its saltiness when it touched our lips. We would be glistening wet with it in an instant yet be forced to endure the stickiness of it for hours. The training schedule seemed to be scaled to how many gallons of sweat each recruit could manufacture, and those hot, paved grinders aided in the sweat production division of the Corps. If the Marines could develop a method of turning that sweat into fuel, they could run the Seventh Fleet for six months off one summer recruit platoon.

If anyone screwed up on the grinder, even there the DI would hand out 340 discipline, after a quick glance around to ensure the absence of passing autos or strangers. A quick, secluded slap in the midst of the platoon was commonplace, and while it was apparent enough to the recipient, it went relatively unnoticed by most of the other recruits. It now seems incredible that I could have been so nonchalant about something so serious.

Since I'd had some military training in close-order drill in high school, I knew the basic movement in formations. Of course, I was only an infant in the eyes of the DIs, even though they saw that I knew the basics. Still, once I came under fire from Egge for, of all things, turning to my left when I should have turned right. That was a stupid thing for a person with prior training to do.

Egge hit me with a verbal barrage as I quickly faced the proper direction. In typical form, he shrieked, "What in hell are you doing, Moore?"

I started to answer, "Sir, I . . . "

"No excuse, Dumbass!" he interrupted, "And you've got some military background! Jesus Christ! Put your brain in a matchbox and it'd be like a B-B in a boxcar!" If I hadn't been so scared, I'd have laughed at that one. I've used it in jest myself since I left the Corps. That one and another Egge used: "Put your brain on the edge of a razor blade and it'd be like a B-B in the middle of an eight-lane highway!" Funny, as I look back. Right then, though, I wasn't sure what was next from Egge, but he must have been in one of his better moods as he simply growled in my face, "You'd best snap out of it and get with the program!"

"Sir, yes, Sir!" I replied, relieved to get off with such a light reprimand and determined to keep a closer watch on my concentration in the future.

The grinder was also used for practice by an entire series when we rehearsed for the parades and inspections which would come towards the end of our basic training. At those times, an officer or two would usually be around and the DIs were more verbal than physical, which was a welcome relief. I'll never know how we kept from wearing out the pavement of those grinders, or at the very least from leaving permanent heel marks in the asphalt for all those who would follow to see.

The author at about the fifth week of basic training.

New recruits arriving at the Recruit Receiving Center.

The armorer assigns each recruit an M-14.

Recruits on the grinder.

*Ransom Downes,
the author's smoking
partner, in
the squad bay.*

*Author on the rifle range during
final qualification week.*

Recruits running the obstacle course.

Ladder obstacle on the confidence course.

Pugil stick fighting.

(listed alphabetically)

Angione, Frank G.
Barber, David A.
Boggs, James R.
Brandt, William M.
Burke, John R.
Cahill, William L.
Caldwell, John L.
Cheetham, Donald F.
Codega, Richard A.
Coleman, Ronald L.
Cooper, Robert J.
Creech, John S., Jr.
Crogan, Kenneth D.
Crowder, Robert L.
Cruz, Marvin
Currid, Patrick J.
Daunno, Valentino J.

Downes, Ransom H., Jr.
Duggins, Roger W.
Felici, Ronald M.
Finnegan, Gerald
Frey, John J.
Fuentes, Alde A.
Geist, Raymond P., Jr.
Goldberg, Harvey E.
Goncalo, Robert M.
Gracia, Joffre Jr.
Guisewhite, Terry L.
Herlihy, Donald E.
Hoffman, Michael S.
Hyle, Kenneth P.
Irvine, W. Jamie T.
Johnson, Sherman R.
Kidwell, James L.

Krepps, David K.
Krout, Philip E.
Lamb, Johnny E., Jr.
McClure, Robert A.
McNally, Daniel T.
Mello, John III
Menezes, Herbert J.
Mezzone, Robert G.
Moore, Herbert L., Jr.
Mutz, Martin L., Jr.
Nicosia, Paul D.
O'Brien, James R.
O'Byrne, Emmet
O'Keefe, John D.
Palmer, William
Parker, John D.
Patrie, Dennis R.

Pender, Ronald D.
Preuss, Roger E.
Rich, William W.
Salvo, Rhett W.
Siebold, Frederick P.
Silvia, Garrett W.
Sims, Richard J.
Smelcer, George A.
Smith, Desmond J.
Souza, William J.
Spanbauer, Richard J.
Spaulding, John E.
Stark, Jerold E.
Walsh, John M.
Willard, Stephen H.
Yates, Gene W.
Egge, Sgt. Walter B., Senior DI

PALMER, 1st row, 3rd from right
AUTHOR, 2nd row, 1st on left
KIDWELL, 2nd row, 2nd from left
WILLARD, 2nd row, 8th from left
GOLDBERG, 4th row, 3rd from right
RICH, 5th row, 1st on left

MUTZ, 5th row, 3rd from left
CAHILL, 5th row, 7th from left
HERLIHY, 5th row, 8th from left
PENDER, 5th row, 5th from right
DOWNES, 5th row, 4th from right

HOUCHINS, GERALD W. - Absent on emergency leave when platoon picture taken.

Sgt. Walter B. Egge, right, Senior Drill Instructor of Platoon 340. Egge, below, instructs a recruit on the rifle range.

Photo courtesy American Yearbook

*A DI
inspects the
author's M-14.*

*The author
wearing a
chrome dome
outside his
barracks.*

Elliott's Beach. Assembling the M-14 blindfolded.

*Sgt. Egge receiving trophy for Platoon 340's
winning obstacle course competition.*

Photos courtesy American Yearbook Co.

Elliott's Beach. Evening skits by trainees.

The Boot, the trophy 340 won in The Drill Competition.

Final Field Inspection. Above (left to right): Rich, Cahill, McNally, Herlihy and Downes. Below: the author.

Graduation Day. The author is at center. From left to right: his future mother-in-law; fiancée, Kathy; his mother; and future sister-in-law, Sharon.

Twenty years later: The author with his wife, Kathy, and sons Jeffrey, age seven, and Gregory, age four. Below: The main gate to Parris Island. Note the "Visitors Welcome" sign.

Photo courtesy American Yearbook Co.

XI

RIFLE RANGE

XI

B Y THE SIXTH OR SEVENTH week of our training, just prior to our move to the Rifle Range, I realized that a new dimension was shaping itself somewhere inside me. I had endured the abuses and punishments. I had felt the physical pain and the emotional stress. The change was in my ability to endure and my attitude about the abuses. The fist in the stomach didn't hurt as much, and emotional stresses had become a basic reality. Part of the ability to accept the physical punishment would have to be attributed to my increased stamina and conditioning resulting from the rigid exercise program, but the mental perception of the abuses probably accounted for most of the newly acquired resistance to pain. When I could see that a fist was imminent, I was able to block the pain in my mind, at the same time tightening the stomach muscles.

Most of 340 adjusted to the pain, but I never dreamed I one day would be able to stand rigidly at the position of attention and experience a fist in the stomach without flinching or moving—or showing in any outward manner that I had received the blow. But I did. And others in 340 later told me that they, too, had shared that same experience. The body can take far more abuse than I had previously thought, and the mind can accept a forced change of environment, contrary to all its past knowledge, once the ability to control that environment is placed in someone else's hands. On the one hand, it was miraculous to see and experience that ability, but on the other hand, it seemed a tragedy to expose the body and the mind to those horrible nightmares.

The weeks passed slowly, each day etched in our minds through hard work and sweat. There appeared to be no end to our daily dose of harassment and discipline. Even during the sixth and seventh week simple pleasures weren't permitted. No radio, TV, newspapers or magazines were available. Events outside the Island were reported only in fragmented notes in letters from home. One of only a few times during that summer I ever stepped into an air-conditioned room was when I went to have some dental work done.

Since each minute of our day was allocated to Marine Corps instruction, and each night to preparing for the next day's tasks, I fantasized about sitting in an air-conditioned room in a soft easy chair with my feet propped up, absorbed in only total silence. I imagined that the room was closed to all others and I could just sit back, close my eyes and relax, with no screaming DIs and with time to do just as I pleased, if I pleased. What's the old saying about simple pleasures being the best?

On August 4, we packed up all our gear and personal items and moved to the rifle range, a distance of about a mile and a half. Our new home for the next three weeks would be a pre-World War II wooden barracks.

These barracks were built in the shape of an "H". The platoons lived in the wings represented by the uprights of the "H", with one platoon upstairs and one downstairs on either end.

That was the only time our whole series was together in one building while we were in training. The cross member of the "H" housed the company offices and DIs' houses as well as supply closets and latrines. The hardwood floors squeaked and moaned under the constant strain of running recruits.

We were each issued a cotton twill shooting jacket with a padded shoulder and elbow that caused more body heat and sweat, as we were soon to discover. Also, we were issued several more empty magazines for our M-14s, to be used later when we started to fire our rifles. Until then, we had only carried the rifles around on our shoulders, practicing the manual of arms, and had received no firing instructions. We had even walked guard duty with empty rifles. Not that our lives and property were particularly endangered, since we only guarded places like our barracks, the mess hall and a few other buildings on a base that was essentially closed to the public.

True to Marine Corps doctrines, we set in on a field day to clean the barracks as an introduction to our three-week stay on the rifle range. We found that cleaning the wood floors was a much harder task than that of cleaning the concrete floors of the barracks we moved from, since the wood floors had small cracks between each board where sand collected. The DIs had us repeat the floor cleaning several times before it passed their inspection. The monsters did show up, but not as raging monsters so much as grouchy old bears. Several hours later, after all the scrubbing, the squad bay looked as though we had been there for weeks. The remainder of that weekend was spent on P.T., eating, playing games, sleeping and going to classes introducing us to the three weeks to follow on the range.

Marines pride themselves on their ability to fire accurately. At first, I felt that spending one-fourth of our time on the range sounded abnormally long. Well, not so. The first week is spent learning the correct firing position for each of the four stances required to qualify. Included in this learning process, aside from the classes, is the exercise of "snapping-in," the procedure for practicing each firing position with an empty rifle, all the while holding the weapon in the correct position to strengthen arm and shoulder muscles. Snapping-in was, to be polite, a pain in the neck. Baked by the white-hot August sun, we snapped-in on the ground in those hot jackets until every muscle in our arms and shoulders would cramp.

Out at the range we wore soft hats, much like soft cotton baseball caps, instead of the chrome domes. That made the sun seem even hotter, and we irrigated yet another portion of the Island with our sweat. Hour after hour we would snap-in, ever watchful of the DIs who patrolled, checking each recruit to see that he correctly followed the range instructor's orders.

Our range instructor was a slow-talking Southern sergeant about thirty-eight or forty years old. He was a dedicated instructor, always repeating and demonstrating any point necessary to help a recruit prepare for the final act of this phase of training—qualifying with his rifle. To qualify, a Marine must score 188 points out of a possible 250, a perfect score and a feat never yet accomplished. A score from 188 to 212 is classified as a "marksman." From 213 to 220 is classified a "sharpshooter" and an "expert" is from 220 to 250.

The distance of targets varies with the firing position. The standing position, called off-hand, is fired at a distance of two hundred yards; for the prone position, or lying on your stomach, the distance is five hundred yards. From the three-hundred-yard position, you fire from the sitting and kneeling position. The bull's-eye is a twelve-inch black circle for the two- and three-hundred-yard positions, and from the five-hundred-yard prone position, the bull's-eye is twenty inches. The recruit must also shoot "rapid" fire from both the two- and three-hundred-yard distances.

Shooting a specific number of rounds, usually ten, at the targets in a specific amount of time, usually a minute, is known as rapid fire shooting. The target for rapid fire is not a round bull's-eye but a rough silhouette of the head and shoulders of a man. Rapid fire from two hundred yards is done from the sitting position, while from three hundred yards it is fired from the prone position.

For qualification, we had to shoot ten shots each from the off hand, sitting and kneeling, prone, rapid fire sitting, and rapid fire prone positions. A bull's-eye counted five points, the next outer ring, or circle, counted four points, the next ring was three points, with the outermost ring two points. These concentric circles were about six inches apart. Simply to qualify, or meet what the Marines consider the lowest level of competence, as I've stated, a minimum of 188 points is required. This means that for every ten shots fired, more than seven have to hit the bull's-eye. Sound easy? Well let me put it another way. From five hundred yards, that twenty-inch bull's-eye appears the size of a piece of pencil lead held at about arm's length from your face. Add to this the wind variable and you have a complicated formula which allows very little room for error.

Since these demands to qualify are stressed so thoroughly in the Corps, it was a pleasant surprise to find that Egge, Rast and Thomson backed off ever so slightly in their monster attacks, and instead, channeled their efforts into helping each man qualify. You can be sure the harassment didn't stop, only slacked off. They still had to maintain control. Sometimes they developed other tactics to accomplish a goal, such as the nightly "traveling minstrel" shows they put us through during the last two weeks on the range.

The night following a day's firing, platoon members who had not fired the minimum score of 188 were marched around to other platoon squad bays with their clothes on backwards. The nonqualifiers, called "UNQs" or "Uneks," sang songs about how they were unable to fire their rifles. Their embarrassment was obvious. Dirty jobs were also assigned to them as incentive to qualify. Many nights, I thanked God I didn't have to travel with the minstrels.

One of the recruits who had to participate in most of the

minstrel shows was Gerry Houchins from Orlando, Florida. Houchins had reported to Parris Island weighing less than a hundred and thirty pounds, but as a result of the healthy diet and exercise had gained about thirty or thirty-five pounds of hard muscle. As an outdoorsman and hunter for years before joining the Marines, he was familiar with firearms and an excellent shot; yet his scores on the range seemed to contradict that fact.

Before firing, Houchins was careful to check and double check the proper elevation and windage settings on his M-14. He conscientiously followed instructions to ensure correct posture for each firing position. Everything seemed to be proper, except his score. He could not make the qualifying score of 188 no matter how he tried. Each night that Rast was on duty, Houchins could look forward to more than just the minstrel show. Rast would punch him in the stomach as he chewed him out for his inability to qualify. That only put more pressure on Houchins for the next day, and each day brought us closer to the final trial of qualification day. The future did not look bright for the recruit.

Houchins had enlisted in the USMC Reserve, and had been a member long enough to have been issued some of his utility uniforms and boots before he left for Parris Island. In those days, one could enlist in the Reserves and spend up to a year attending the monthly drills before reporting for basic training. That way, an individual could actually receive credit for his Reserve time while on active duty, and both Reserve and active duty were included when calculating when his enlistment was over. Houchins had worn his utility uniforms to those weekend drills for a sufficient period that they had become faded from repeated washings. There is an epithet in the Corps for someone who has been a Marine long enough for his utility uniforms to acquire that faded look: "salty." Often as not, he also acquires somewhat of a swagger in his walk in his effort to exude a picture of self-confidence. ("Cocky" might be the civilian equivalent.) "Salty" is a word reserved only for those who have earned it, and it's unforgivable for a recruit to try to project that image.

Houchins did not possess any of the qualities of a salty Marine except that his combat uniforms were faded. For some reason, Thomson reacted adversely to Houchins' appearance. He would approach Houchins and growl, "You gettin' salty on me, Sweetheart?" and before Houchins could reply, Thomson would hit him in the stomach, or slap him on the head. I don't know how many times Houchins was struck by Thomson for this, but a conservative estimate would be that it occurred at least three times a week.

So Houchins was getting beatings from Thomson for the "salty routine," and from Rast for not qualifying on the rifle range. Each time I saw Houchins taking his 340 discipline, I sympathized with him, but I could only be thankful that it was not me. In what now seems bizarre behavior to me, I felt a tinge of relief when somone clse was punishcd. Since the DI was occupied with chastising another recruit, the rest of us felt "safe," at least for the duration of the punishment.

On the Friday of qualification, Houchins' scores had not improved and the stress was obviously wearing on him. He approached the firing line as he had each previous day—confident and ready. This day, as usual, Thomson was watching closely as Houchins fired the first several shots. After each shot, Thomson inquired where Houchins thought he had hit the target. His response was the same every time, "Right there, Sir," meaning he thought he had hit the bull's-eye. Each time though, the red flag would pass across the target signifying a miss.

In a gesture which almost defined the word despair, Thomson finally gave an order to Houchins: "Clear that weapon and bring it with you." He spun on his heels and started towards the range armorer with Houchins close behind. Upon checking the rifle, the armorer discovered that the weapon had a malfunctioning rear sight. Each time the rifle fired, the elevation knob would drop several clicks, rendering the next shot even farther off the mark! Houchins' poor score was a result of a defective weapon rather than lack of expertise on his part.

To make matters worse, the rifle could not be repaired out on the range. Thomson made arrangements for Houchins to use another recruit's rifle to attempt to complete the qualification firing, but all the initial seven or eight shots that missed would have to be included in his score. Houchins would not be permitted to shoot those over. Although these had taken about 40 points off Houchins' score already, the range officer ruled that Houchins would have to live with it. That left Houchins with 42 shots to score 188 points, which meant that out of 42 shots remaining, he had to hit the bull's-eye 38 times merely to qualify in the lowest category. To the surprise of more than a few people, though, he did qualify! And he did so using a rifle he was firing for the first time.

Rifle range life was basically hours upon hours of hard, tedious work dedicated to acquiring the M-14 skills. Evenings were spent in the daily ritual of cleaning the weapon thoroughly. The procedure even called for us to take the metal parts of the rifle into the showers to scrub and clean with hot water, and then to dry out the parts, oil them and reassemble the rifle. One of the DIs was on hand to inspect the finished product. The Marines, step by step, were slowly welding each recruit and his rifle into a single piece of equipment almost incapable of function when separated.

In the process of training on the range, our schedule was interrupted one afternoon for a most unusual diversion—a volleyball game! To appreciate how this triviality could be considered such an important event, you'll have to recall that we, up until then, had essentially no intraplatoon competitions, games or training tests.

The volleyball game was played on a clay court behind the range mess hall. Several such courts were there as well as an obstacle course and P.T. field. Rast was on duty that day and we split up into teams, pitting one squad against the other. I don't remember who won, but I do remember that we yelled at, and with, one another during the whole contest. There were two games to start with, and the victorious squads met in a final game. The two losing squads stood by and urged on their favorite in the final. We probably broke most of the rules of competition, but it was an enjoyable game and a welcome diversion in our schedule. Laughter erupted a few times. Even Rast seemed to enjoy our competition, and it ended all too soon for us.

While we were on the rifle range, the DIs let us sing cadence songs as we marched, an outlet for energy we had never been permitted before. The songs were sung to the old tunes I'm sure you've either participated in as a member of the military or heard in movies with military settings. The only difference is the words. Since we were now approaching the latter stages of our training, we counted the days in some of those verses. I remember one went like this:

Twenty-six days left for us, Honey, Honey
Twenty-six days left for us, Babe, Babe
Twenty-six days left for us,
Where the hell's that Greyhound bus,
Honey, oh, Babe be mine—Go to your left, your right,
    your left,
Go to your left . . . .

Another one had the same melody but the punch lines went: "Twenty-six days and we leave here, / Sit on our ass and guzzle beer." Some had some not-so-nice things to say about the DIs, such as "Sergeant Egge's turning green, / Somebody pissed in his canteen." Some got even grosser.

We also saw a couple of movies while we were at the range. The films were shown on a portable screen set up in the mess hall and the DIs scowled the whole time. I remember the first one was a western but I can't recall the plot. Some of the films were strictly Marine Corps propaganda films, such as actual combat footage of the battles of Iwo Jima and Tarawa. We weren't provided with films of Elizabeth Taylor or other beautiful actresses in compromising attire.

One of the simple pleasures I found a way to indulge in was in direct conflict with the instructions of the DIs. I smoked before coming to the Island but that privilege was taken away by the DIs. When we first went to the PX as a platoon to get our personal hygiene and health care products, all those who smoked were permitted to purchase a carton of cigarettes. We had no money, so they charged our purchases and withheld the sum from our first pay check. (I've kept that receipt, and it amounted to thirty-seven dollars and some change.) I bought a carton of Winstons and carried them back to the barn, only to have Egge advise us of the no-smoking rule until we earned the privilege.

Ransom Downes also smoked and had purchased cigarettes. Week after week those cigarettes went unopened, lying in full view in my locker box. Downes and I came up with the idea of having the firewatch wake us at 2:00 a.m. so we could sneak a smoke in the latrine. We opened one of the packs from the bottom and slipped out two cigarettes, replaced the pack in the carton and puffed away. We never told anybody about this treasured, twenty-minute pleasure, much like the ecstasy of two young country boys stealing a smoke behind the barn. The excitement of the forbidden probably heightened the experience more than the joy of smoking.

Downes and I continued these smoking sessions out on the rifle range but we had to change tactics. Instead of smoking in the latrine, which on the range was next to the DI's house, we would slip outside in the humid night air, crawl under one of the large oleander bushes which grew about fifty feet behind the barracks and smoke blissfully, more often than not without speaking, until we grew tired or were smoked out. Then we would sneak back into the barracks, slip into our bunks and sleep soundlessly until wake-up call. I can still picture the feeling of tranquility—lying under that oleander, watching the smoke drift up through the leaves towards the flickering stars of the clear summer night. I don't know that I've ever before or since enjoyed a cigarette so much. One night we were under the oleander smoking away when the sound of the fire alarm shattered the still night air. For a second or two we weren't sure what to do. We couldn't get back inside to exit with the platoon, but we certainly couldn't stay where we were, as the DIs would check the platoon by having us count off to make sure all had evacuated. Downes and I both had visions of impending doom if Rast caught us outside. As fate would have it, in the confusion of the series vacating the building, our platoon came pouring out the door right in front of the oleander where we were hiding. In the darkness, we crawled out from under the bush and fell into our positions in the platoon formation, our hearts pumping away from fear of apprehension. Rast didn't catch us and our secret was safe. We didn't make it out to the oleander for several days.

The first two weeks on the range came to an end and the big week, qualification time, was at hand. We all felt confident about our ability, and progress was evident in our skills. Chests out and leaning back as we strutted, we marched around the range singing the usual ditties, "Lift your head and hold it high, 340 is passing by," etc. We looked good when we strutted to impress the passengers of slowly passing cars, and Egge at last could be proud of us. We had taken on the aura of a budding senior platoon. Did I say senior platoon? Already? Well, almost. Although we were a week away from getting the flag with the fringe, it was still difficult to picture ourselves under that flag. One step at a time! One foot in front of the other! Egge's law. Don't quit.

The final week on the range began on a typical hot and humid August Monday. We now rehearsed daily the firing sequence and positions we would use on Friday, final qualification day. All our efforts were now directed at hitting the bull's-eye. Each day the strain of cramped and tired muscles would remind us of the task ahead. Range instructors and DIs passed among us, checking to see if we had noted the latest wind direction in our score books. The singing while we marched continued, but it took on a more serious undercurrent, a sense of purpose to our efforts. A quiet determination crept over the whole platoon. Each day's firing practice took on new significance. We all felt the pressure, DIs included.

Friday arrived clear and hot, the sky a deep blue with only puffs of white clouds. We were all relieved that it was not a cloudy, windy day, knowing that the treacherous winds on the Island could wreak havoc with our scores. Anxiously, we went through the rituals of counting off, a short run, breakfast, and the final inspection of our rifles, checking ever so carefully the correct settings on the sights and securing the slings for proper fit. Egge, Rast and Thomson were all there that Friday. It was too important to miss. A final deep breath and we fell outside to march across the road to the range.

There were not enough targets for the whole platoon to shoot simultaneously, so we fired in three relays. While the first relay approached the firing line, the second sat on empty ammo boxes about ten yards behind the line; the third relay, another ten yards back, sat on long wooden benches much like those along the sidelines of a football field. A blackboard on a portable tripod stood between the firing line and the recruits of the second relay and was manned by an official Marine Corps scorer. I fired on the first relay on target No. 9. I would use the same target for each position and shoot with the same relay, thereby allowing the scorer to record my score at one position, and when we moved back to the next distance, he had the same recruit shooting in the same sequence. Our scores were recorded after each shot for all to see, although each of us was too concerned with his task at hand to worry about how another recruit fared.

As I approached the firing line at the two-hundred-yard marker, I had adjusted my sling for the off-hand position and rechecked, for the final time, the sight adjustments for distance and wind. I still have my scoring booklet where I recorded twenty-two clicks of elevation and one click left for windage that day. It was only about nine o'clock in the morning but the sun blasted down on us, and as usual sweat poured freely—that day as much from anxiety as from heat. The scorer handed me my first ten cartridges, the brass already hot from the sun. I stepped up to the small marker placed on the ground, took one last deep breath and waited.

From a small, hand-held bullhorn came the voice of the range officer repeating the words every Marine has heard for generations on the rifle range, "All ready on the left?" Short pause. "All ready on the right?" Another pause. Then, "All Ready on the firing line! Watch your targets!" That was our cue that the time had come for us to take matters in our own hands. From now until the final shot at five hundred yards, there would be no one to help if we couldn't perform. Training was over. This one was for the record.

As target No. 9 was raised to its full height, I loaded the rifle with a single cartridge. I lifted the M-14, feeling the now-comfortable grip of the sling as I pulled the rifle into my shoulder. I tried to summon all the lessons of the range instructor as I let rifle settle down on the black bull's-eye on the white background target two hundred yards away. The range instructor's words were easy to recall. "Remember the word BRASS," he had told us, in his Southern accent: "The letters tell you to Breath . . . Relax . . . Aim . . . Slack . . . Squeeze!" I followed his instructions, although the relaxing part had been eaiser before today. I mentally had to repeat the "squeeze" for a third time before the now familiar explosion of the rifle firing filled my ears.

Immediately, target No. 9 disappeared. "Good," I thought, "at least I hit the target on my first shot!" Another thirty seconds of agonized waiting and the target was raised again. The smell of powder from the freshly spent cartridge was thick as I waited to see where I had struck the target. My heart jumped—no, it fairly leaped—as I saw the white disc raised signifying a bull's-eye. With each shot that followed, it became more of the practiced routine of days past, with each man applying his past two and a half weeks' training lessons. The rest of the qualifying round that morning doesn't stand out in my mind, only the events leading up to, and the results of, that first shot. I ended up qualifying almost before we had to shoot from the five-hundred-yard distance.

By the time all three relays had finished firing, I recall Egge's telling us we had qualified ninety percent of the platoon. That had not suited Egge and the other DIs, as they had wanted, of course, a hundred percent qualification. As it turned out, we finished second in total number of qualified recruits in our series, so by those standards we lost the series rifle range competition. Still, those three weeks on the range had been beneficial. We found that we could take instructions and put them to the test. Each man had faced that test and ninety percent had passed!

That Friday afternoon we were all assembled, the whole series, for the awarding of our qualification badges. Officers also presented the award for the highest score fired by a recruit, who happened to be Mutz from 340. That won him a set of PFC stripes and softened the blow to Egge's ego somewhat. The rifle range was over! The pressure to qualify was behind us and the final phase of training was ahead. The pace was to quicken, as we soon found out.

XII

THE OTHER SIDE OF THE MONSTER

XII

WHILE CORPORAL PUNISHMENT was administered by all three DIs in 340, we were to find there was a human side of each of them that we hadn't known existed. Each had shown his ability to perform, both by leadership and by force, and yet there were times when neither of those methods would apply. Sometimes "the book" just wouldn't work. When that time came, the measure of a man was accomplished by his actions.

We had been on the Island about five weeks and had gotten used to the routine. One morning during this time, I think it was a Saturday, Rast had spent the night in the DI's house. As usual, he woke us with the flashing lights and his greeting, "Get up! Get up! It's another glorious day in the Marine Corps, where every day's a holiday and every meal a banquet!"

We snapped to attention at the foot of our racks. Rast started walking slowly down the center aisle as he roared, "Count . . . off!" We started the morning ritual in the same manner we had each morning since our arrival. The count went down one side of the squad bay, then back up the other. I had noticed nothing odd about that particular morning's performance, but Rast had reached only the halfway point in his walk down the squad bay by the time the last recruit sounded off. Rast stopped, turned around and yelled, "Again!"

"Oh, hell," I remember thinking, "it's going to be one of those days." I bent down, touching my toes, while waiting for the count to reach me. I snapped to attention at the precise moment I was supposed to, counted off and remained locked in that position until the full platoon had completed the task.

Thomson was just arriving, having come up the stairs the DIs used at the back of the barracks. Rast was striding toward the DI's house when he met Thomson. "We've got a bug-out!" Rast said, the tension of the occasion registering in his voice.

I hadn't even noticed that the reason Rast had us repeat the counting off was we were one man short. "Bug-out" is the term used by the Corps to designate a recruit who attempts an escape from the Island. There was a flurry of activity as Rast went downstairs to report the missing recruit to the Company Office and call the MPs. We stayed at the position of attention until he returned to the squad bay. The previous night's firewatch roster was checked and each recruit who had been on duty that night was questioned to determine approximately what time the recruit fled.

After the interrogation of the firewatch, we fell outside for the morning run. Upon its completion, we went to the mess hall for breakfast. During the meal, all our thoughts were of the recruit who attempted to escape, though presently I don't remember which recruit was missing. He was trying something we all felt like doing at one time or another. The rest of us had rejected that thought, however. Now, he had the Parris Island MPs after him. With all the animosity about "bug-outs" expressed by the DIs, I wouldn't have traded places with that recruit for anything. Nope, I'd take my chances with 340.

After breakfast, we returned to the barn to find that Egge also had arrived. That didn't really surprise me, but what I saw next did. The bug-out's equipment, clothes, rifle and 782 gear was gone. His bunk had been stripped of blanket, sheets and pillow case. It looked as though no one had ever slept there. Glances were exchanged among us recruits about what we saw, but as usual, no talking. We still weren't permitted that luxury.

We never heard another word about the bug-out. Nothing. The DIs did not tell us if he was caught, if he was in jail, if he escaped—nothing. Each of us knew that if he was caught he would be sent down to "motivation" to be evaluated and "treated." At any rate, we knew he probably would never see 340 again.

It is military policy to grant emergency leave to a recruit who has a death in his family. Unless the emergency is of such magnitude, a recruit will find it all but impossible to get official leave from the training schedule. It is necessary to know that in order to understand fully the implications of the events of that weekend.

We returned to the barn in the late afternoon after firing for record and going through the awards ceremony. A messenger came to our squad bay and told Rast that I had an emergency phone call. (Only an emergency can get a recruit to the phone.) I was told to call the number scribbled on a slip of paper Rast handed me. The closest phone was a pay booth on the street down from our barracks. Since a recruit has no money, Rast gave me a dime and told me to make the long distance call to Charleston, collect.

I had known immediately upon seeing the number that I was to call my fiancée, Kathy. My future father-in-law answered and informed me that Kathy's grandmother, his mother-in-law, had died. She was a wonderful woman and I had grown to love her as a member of my own family during the seven years I had been dating her granddaughter. Letters from Kathy had told me she was gravely ill, yet the news was still a shock. I explained that I didn't think there was any way I could get home for the funeral, expressed my sorrow at her death, and, with a hollow feeling in my stomach, returned to the squad bay.

I reported back to Rast, who had a serious look of concern in his eyes as he asked what the problem was. After he had taken me into the DI's house and closed the door, I explained what the phone call had been about. He asked if we, Kathy's grandmother and I, had been close, and I explained my feelings to him. He told me in a quiet, personable voice to go back to my rack and get things squared away for the move back to our Third Battalion barn tomorrow.

Later that evening, Rast called me back to the DI's house, where he again closed the door and informed me that arrangements had been made for me to attend the funeral in Charleston on Saturday. He advised me to pack all my gear and have it ready for the move, and informed me that since I had no civilian clothing, I would have to obtain a dress uniform for the trip. He arranged for me to go with him to get clothing first thing in the morning while the rest of the platoon moved back to the old barn.

Rast escorted me over to supply and I was fitted with a new summer dress uniform. He then took me back over to the Third Battalion offices where I was met by Kathy and her father. A liberty pass, good until five o'clock the next day, Sunday, was given to me and we left for Charleston.

It was late August as we left the Island for the funeral, and I had become somewhat accustomed to the spartan life of a recruit in training. As Kathy, her father and I drove the seventy-five miles back to Charleston, I had mixed feelings. This was not time for me to tell of my problems, and I had a genuine sorrow over the task at hand. I didn't talk much about what was going on at the Island. I didn't know what would happen to me when I returned if I talked too much about the abuses, so I minimized them, at least for that short time.

We went to Kathy's home, where I shared in the grief of the

family's loss, and then left to go to my own home only a few miles away. I drove over myself and the luxury of being alone was in itself a shock to my senses. Instead of driving straight to the house, I drove around for another ten or fifteen minutes, soaking up the reality of having no DIs or anyone to tell me what I could or could not do. I stopped at a local gas station and bought a Coke from the vending machine. Such a trivial act may not appear to be important in the day-to-day activities of most people, but to a recruit going through the disciplined life of Parris Island, it represented a freedom of choice and action not ordinarily experienced. I clearly remember thinking about how naive most of us are about the events taking place around us. The typical person driving up and down that road knew nothing about what was happening on the Island only seventy-five miles away. The majority of them could not have cared less. Many would never know. They were untouched by the present circumstances affecting my life.

I got back in the car for the short drive to my home. I was warmly embraced by my mother and younger brother, Bill, and became the target of the expected questions of a concerned mother: "Are you eating enough?" "Are you getting enough sleep?" "Are they too rough?" My brother, only eight at the time, could only relate to the uniform. His eyes were wide with joy at having a brother who was, at least in his small eyes, a real Marine. He couldn't keep his hands off my rifle qualification badge and insisted on wearing my hat around the house, playing happily with that symbol of "his" accomplishments as a "Marine." My mother's joy at having me home, even for a short time, was evident in her enthusiastic hug as I entered the house, and continued as she kept before me an array of my favorite foods and beverages. I had forgotten how good her iced tea was, and how good air conditioning could feel. If it had not been for the solemn occasion of my visit, the weekend would have been one of sheer joy at being away from the perplexities and indignities of the Island.

The funeral was scheduled for the early afternoon, and beforehand I ate a ham and cheese sandwich and drank what seemed to be two gallons of iced tea. I decided to shower again before the funeral, and was almost startled when I walked into a colorful bathroom scented with spiced soap placed in a small ornamental dish. Funny how a smell can activate so many emotions, but right then I remembered nights of preparing for a date, or special dance or party in that same room, surrounded by these same fragrances. As I showered, I realized this was the first time I had showered alone in more than two months. With no one to harass me, I stood soaking up the sheer delight of a leisurely shower. As I dried off with a soft, fluffy, figured towel, again the past flooded my mind. It all seemed so far away and long ago. Even then I couldn't rid my thoughts of the Island. I wondered what 340 was doing right at that moment, and I had a small attack of the guilts. Here I was casually taking a shower in the middle of the afternoon simply because I wanted to, and 340 was probably having a field day or maybe "watching TV." I quickly ejected those thoughts from my mind and dressed for the funeral.

In preparing to leave, I looked in the mirror and was somewhat taken aback. Maybe it was because I had never seen a recruit in that mirror before, only a teenager with frivolous things to do and places to go; now a stranger was staring back at me. No longer did I have a full head of hair, and the uniform looked strange. The deeply tanned face was familiar, but the look in the eyes was different. I couldn't even be certain just what had changed. I stood looking at that reflection a short time longer, again thinking of 340. "Damn!" I thought, "Why can't I forget all that for a day or two?" Rast had told me not to be seen out of uniform or without my liberty pass. It never occurred to me that I could have worn a suit and tie to the funeral. Who would have known? Or cared? But I didn't; I followed Rast's instructions to the letter. I put my pass in my pocket and left to pick up Kathy for the funeral.

When we arrived at the funeral home, most of Kathy's family were already there. We walked up to the casket to look at her grandmother one last time. I looked down at the frail figure in the coffin and felt that in death she looked peaceful, with no signs of the pain she had suffered in her final days. The white satin pillow and profusion of flowers lent an air of tranquility to her last rites and I felt remorse at not having been able to see her before she died. Outside, before the service began, I casually conversed with family members, taking their half-hearted comments about the Marines in stride, knowing that it was simply small talk to distract them from the occasion at hand.

The service was not a long one, which was as it should be, and I could not keep my mind on the words of the minister. Death is never an easy thing for survivors to cope with. The feeling of personal loss was understood and shared by all present. A light touch or a soft caress communicated our shared emotions.

After the service in the small chapel, we drove to the cemetery outside the small town of Walterboro, a forty-five minute drive from Charleston. Another short rite was held at the graveside. The cemetery was a small, old one, nestled under several ancient moss-draped oak trees and punctuated with mossy tombstones dating back to the mid-eighteen hundreds. It was peaceful and quiet, with only the sounds of an occasional car passing on the nearby road. Unspoken last respects were said by us all, after which we returned to Charleston.

That night Kathy and I went to a movie. The movie house had a significant impact on my senses. I had forgotten, truly forgotten, how all-encompassing air conditioning could be. It not only felt refreshingly cool, it even smelled cool! The cool dark surroundings could not have been appreciated by anyone more than I. And hot, buttered popcorn! I hadn't thought about that, not since June. I ate popcorn until I was desperate for a Coke, which was conveniently at hand! Cool air, popcorn, Coke and Kathy. If 340 could have seen me then!

After I took Kathy home that night, I went by the local drive-in restaurant where my old friends and schoolmates were making their final rounds of the night. I sat and drank a cold beer (one of only two that night) with friends since it was nearing the 1:00 a.m. closing time. I was almost asleep on my feet since my system had become accustomed to going to sleep hours earlier. I told a few of my old football teammates of my experiences on the Island, but they were skeptical that the things I described truly happened. Seeing the obvious disbelief on their faces, I didn't try to convince them. Our worlds of the present were just too far apart. They saw my experience as an adventure while I saw it as survival. I was too tired to explain, and it really wouldn't have changed anything if I had, so I went home.

I arrived home that night to find the light on in my room and the sheets folded down on the wide double bed. I smiled at this small display of my mother's continuing welcome. I turned off the light and remember wondering who had the last firewatch at 340 that night. The steady hum of the central air conditioner put me to sleep almost as soon as I closed my eyes.

Months of waking at four in the morning caused my eyes to pop wide open the next morning at precisely that hour. Before my mind caught up with reality, I bounded out of the bed and stood alone in the darkness of my room. At length, I sat back on the edge of the bed, thinking about where I had come from and when I had to return. Then I lay back down, fully intending to retrieve some of the sleep Parris Island had deprived me of. But I couldn't go back to sleep. My mind drifted from one thought to another as I watched the sky outside come to life. I had put on my watch upon my return home, and when six o'clock came I knew that 340 had probably returned from the mess hall. I was hoping Rast had the weekend off. They were probably settled in at our old barn in Third Battalion now that the rifle range was over. In less than twelve hours, I would be, too.

At breakfast, my father and I talked, but only between the constant outbursts of questions from my brother and the loving interrogation of my mother. My father knew of Parris Island's reputation and, when away from my mother, asked if I had any problems. I minimized the abuses and treatment by the DIs. I've always thought that he saw through my accounts, but he never let on and I've never asked.

We went to church, a lifelong Sunday morning habit, and I renewed my ties with the other side of my family. I felt awkward in the presence of some whom I saw that morning. It was only because I was in uniform, for I had never before been to church feeling improperly dressed. I probably looked different to them, too, with my skinned head shining in the morning light. Older men of the church stopped me after the service to offer heartfelt greetings and wishes for good luck. I nodded my thank-yous and was more than a little glad when we left. "Less than five hours of freedom left," I thought as we left church to go out to eat.

After another air-conditioned meal, we returned home. By then it was time for me to leave, and I made my exit as quickly as I could. My father's handshake was firm, but a soft look of deep concern was apparent in his eyes. My brother could not know the significance of the events taking place around him, but he clung to my neck to tell me good-bye. I knew it would be hardest on my mother, whose tears were freely falling as she hugged me good-bye. In my most confident voice, I assured her, "I'll do fine." We went out back and I started the car and backed out of the driveway. As I pulled away, my family all stood in the driveway, hands over heads, waving good-bye until I was out of sight. I waved my arm high out of the window in a final farewell and headed for Kathy's house. She was going to drive me back to the Island that afternoon.

My future in-laws had become like my own family during the years I had been dating Kathy. I was comfortable in their home and in their presence. I was close to Kathy's younger sister, Sharon, and spent a few extra minutes trying to help her sort out her boyfriend problems. She was sixteen and I was the closest thing she had to a brother, so I listened and tried to help find an answer. A short visit with out-of-town family members who had stayed over in Charleston until today followed, then it was time to leave—another tearful parting.

On the return trip to the Island, I stopped at a small grocery along the highway just before we reached Beaufort to have another Coke before I returned to my "vacation retreat" for the summer. The trip was all too short, and I dreaded seeing the gates to the Island appear as we rounded the last curve and approached the red-and-yellow Marine Corps sign. I drove through the gates and slowly, ever so slowly, drove towards the hell I had dreaded facing all day. We stopped for a short while at a picnic area alongside the road. As I anticipated, good-bye was not easy for either of us. Time did not permit us to linger, so we drove to the Third Battalion and I waved to Kathy as she tearfully drove away. As she disappeared, I was crushed with the realization that I would have no control over my surroundings again until I left on September 11.

I reported in to the Company Commanders office, where a gunnery sergeant scowled at me as I handed the pass over and prepared to head back to the barn. "You're the first man ever to get liberty off this Island as a recruit," he told me. "Your DIs had to take full responsibility that you'd come back." I wasn't aware until long after I left the Island that Rast had been on the phone calling and seeking a way for me to attend the funeral. He had enlisted the help of Egge, who had already gone home, and they had come up with the suggestion of granting me "liberty," practically unheard of for a recruit. Then they had proceeded to call the necessary offices and paved the way for the arrangements. I think it even required the signature of my future father-in-law.

Rast had to be aware of my animosity towards him. That's precisely why I found it hard to believe he would go to any effort, much less the considerable risk he took, to bend the rules to assist me. I never thanked him, since I didn't realize the full significance of his actions at the time. Rast, wherever you are, I'll thank you here for your efforts on my behalf. There have been, I'm sure, other examples of the human side of the DIs. The image of the barrel-chested, hard-nosed, bellowing, rockhard DI could be ruined if too many stories like this were leaked. A little later, another recruit in 340 was faced with the tragedy of a death in his family. Gerry Houchins, the recruit who qualified with another trainee's rifle, received an emergency call much like mine to inform him that his brother had been killed in an automobile accident on Labor Day. Since the death was in his immediate family, Houchins left quickly on emergency leave to return to Florida for the funeral.

As our graduation drew near, Houchins still had not returned. Due to his prolonged absence from the Island, Houchins missed Elliott's Beach, Final Strength Test, Drill Competition, Battalion Commander's Inspection, Final Written Exam and the Regimental Commander's Inspection. Each day his equipment remained hanging on the end of his rack, waiting for someone to remove it from the ranks of 340. The days wore on, but still no Houchins. We all knew he would be set back for missing all the required tests.

Graduation day arrived, but Houchins did not. All of 340 was happy to progress through the graduation exercise and be with family and loved ones on that long-awaited Tuesday. Obviously, little or no thought was given to Houchins. We were all too caught up in the joyous celebrations of the day.

About six or seven o'clock that evening, the door to the squad bay opened and in walked Houchins! He had returned only a few minutes before to Company Headquarters. Upon reporting to the sergeant on duty, the sergeant had told him to wait while he checked with Sergeant Egge. In another of those unsung heroics of DIs, Egge told the sergeant to send Houchins on over to 340; Houchins would leave the Island with us. I don't know how he arranged for Houchins to "pass" all those tests and inspections we had been told were required, but I do know it was accomplished, and he boarded a Greyhound bus to depart with us.

There can be yet another side to the monsters. When a recruit's attitude prevents his performing to Marine Corps standards, his DI decides whether to send him to a motivation training unit, called the Special Training Battalion or STB. STB uses its own special techniques to try and motivate the recruit to adjust to the circumstances confronting him and return him to the regular training schedule. STB uses P.T., movies and lectures in an attempt to instill desire in the trainee to return to regular training. Unfortunately, STB can reinforce the negative side of the recruit's experiences and complicate his problems.

STB may be a necessary evil to the Marine Corps training program, but the psychological damage can be devastating to a recruit who is told he could spend his entire enlistment on the Island. Since the DI makes the decision to send a recruit to STB, that decision can be reached for the wrong reason. Take the recruit who is sent to STB because of his difficulty in holding up under constant stress. His DI can send him away merely to rid himself of a problem. Let somebody else handle him, he may reason, so I can concentrate on other matters at hand. The recruit arrives at STB and finds himself with other men who, rightfully or not, have been termed misfits or problem cases. More PT and games are played. As often as not, those men are unable to rejoin their original platoons and are assigned to a platoon that came to the Island later than they. When, and if, they re-enter the regular training program, they are called "pick-ups," and considered by their DIs one of the few forms of life lower than a recruit. As such, when the pick-up joins the new platoon, he usually is under constant pressure from the DIs and the vicious circle starts again. All of this because the DI either didn't have the time to handle the problem, or preferred to pass the problem on to somebody else so his record of having a good platoon would not be tarnished.

When a recruit is set back, it has a detrimental impact on the whole platoon. Miller, for instance. As I've stated, Miller reported for basic training overweight. Not fat, mind you, just overweight. I didn't know him personally before the Island since he came from a different part of Charleston from myself, so I had no personal knowledge of his background. Miller struggled through the morning run and the never-ending, sweat-filled sessions of P.T. He "watched TV" with us and held his position until his strength could stand no more. He did just as the rest of us at those times—simply fall for an instant, grab a quick breath and try again. Miller fought through the obstacle course and he studied diligently. He would never admit defeat and he never quit.

Miller had an annoying personal habit of repeating an order or instruction in the form of a question to the DIs, to clarify in his mind I suppose, exactly what was expected of him. If the DI would tell Miller, "Do ten push-ups, Miller!" Miller would reply, "Ten push-ups, Sir?" The DI would holler back, "Yes, Miller, ten!" Miller would then acknowledge with the customary "Aye, aye, Sir!" and carry out the order. That ritual took place each time one of the DIs addressed him.

Miller had been one of the recruits who kept up with the platoon on sheer determination and guts. The DIs pushed him physically and mentally in what I interpreted to be harsher and more intense treatment than that of the recruits who were having less difficulty. Miller was usually one of the last of the platoon at the end of a run, huffing and blowing but completing it and not complaining. I did not envy the fact that he was kept under so much pressure. As I recall, Miller was also on a limited diet to assist in losing weight. The food on his tray did not look appetizing and the quantity was scant. Miller never complained.

We were arriving at the level of a senior platoon and Miller had come through a lot. Each of us had at one time or another seen him, covered with dirt and sweat, standing rigidly at attention as one of the DIs instructed him to repeat some task. I remember one time when I gladly would have run the obstacle course for him. Although he was exhausted from the first run, Egge had ordered him to run it again. It was sad to see the look on Miller's face as he replied as usual, "Do it again, Sir?" His breath was short and his words were gasps.

"Again!" Egge yelled.

As was his habit, Miller answered, "Aye, aye, Sir!" and immediately went to the beginning of the course and proceeded to execute Egge's command. As usual, he made it, but not without a struggle.

Not long after that day on the obstacle course, we were in the squad bay in the early afternoon, standing at attention by our racks. Egge was on duty and started down the center aisle. He was right in front of me, less than an arm's length away, when he stopped and called out, "Miller, bring your rifle and get up here!" Before Miller could do or say anything, Egge held his hand in front of his mouth, palm facing out, and whispered quickly in my direction, "My rifle, Sir?" imitating what he knew Miller was going to say.

True to form and habit, Miller shouted back, "My rifle, Sir?"

Egge's hand flashed out and backhanded me in the stomach, not as a disciplinary action but as confirmation of the accuracy of his whispered prediction. He never realized that the blow he had given me caught me totally off guard and took my breath away. He screamed out, "Hell yes, Miller, your rifle!"

Miller acknowledged the order and reported as he was ordered. Egge had returned to the DI's table and I could not hear all the conversation, but I did hear something about "packing seabag" and "leaving." I had no idea what was happening until I saw Miller, seabag over his shoulder and a dejected expression that told it all. He was being set back! He left with one of the DIs and I never saw him again. Egge only told us that he was no longer with 340 and that he was being set back, confirming what I suspected when I saw Miller's face.

Maybe it was because Miller had come with me from Charleston, maybe it was because Miller never gave up, maybe it was because he had taken so much hell from the DIs, but I was demoralized when he was set back. Not just I but all of us. We realized it could have been any one of our group. Miller's best was not good enough to suit somebody, and that somebody represented the Corps. There were recruits still in the barn who had not been pushed physically as hard as Miller, but because of their physiological makeup, simply got by with doing the minimum. It was a sad day and one I'll never forget. The fear of having that scene repeated simply added an additional element of stress to an already heavy load.

XIII

ELLIOTT'S BEACH

XIII

DURING THE LAST PHASE of our training, we went on an overnight march to Elliott's Beach. Don't let the name fool you since it is not what its name implies, at least not for the recruits. Elliott's Beach is on the southwest corner of the island and is covered with thick woods tangled with undergrowth. There is a staging area with the underbrush cleared where recruits congregate under the canopies of huge oak trees, and there are several outdoor class areas and a few old Quonsett huts. Some of the permanently stationed personnel would go for afternoon family picnics or gatherings with friends to a large open field several hundred yards away up the beach side. Adjoining the open field was a playground for children as well as access to the water for swimming. A gentle ocean breeze always blew and families could relax under the shade of the huge oaks or swim or lie in the sun. We would not be concerned with the family area of Elliott's Beach since we were on that part of the Island strictly as part of our basic training.

We had shouldered a full combat field pack complete with clothing and 782 gear, donned our chrome domes, slung our rifles over our shoulders and marched the two or three miles from our barn to the cleared area under the oaks. Egge, Rast and Thomson all made the trip with us and we set in to establish a base camp, with 340 breaking down into two-man pup tent teams. We were taught to place our tents in Marine Corps combat-ready tactical units. For the layman, that simply means we spread out in specified locations as we would if we were in a combat situation. Each tent was five yards or so from the next, and my tentmate was Jimmy Kidwell from Orlando, Florida, Kidwell was about the same height and weight as I, but he had red hair and a full complement of freckles. Each recruit had in his 782 gear half of a two-man tent, and Kidwell and I had no problems in erecting our small squat home for the stay at the beach.

After we had completed setting up our base camp, we began the revered Marine Corps tactical procedure of policing the area. To me, that always seemed a time-killer; since all Marines must clean the area before they leave, why should there anything for new arrivals to police? We walked, bent over with heads bowed, searching thirty minutes for debris or trash, then were called to formation and given a short lecture on our upcoming field maneuvers. Once the lecture was over, we separated into groups to take some of our tests.

These tests varied in importance and difficulty. One of the tests was high on the scale of both of those requisites. Each of us had to put on a blindfold, stand at a waist-high, crudely constructed table and completely fieldstrip (disassemble) the M-14 rifle and reassemble it in a specified time period—to my best recollection, two minutes. That wasn't too difficult when you remember that we had, by then, lived with those M-14s for almost three months, studying and practicing the care, maintenance and operation of each part. The blindfold was added to simulate nighttime, and the time frame was used to stress the urgency of finding and repairing a malfunction in combat, where the life of the Marine may well hinge on his ability to restore quickly his weapon to combat readiness.

The instructors supervising these tests would often complicate the problem by moving a part from where the recruit placed it, relocating it perhaps a foot away. That simple maneuver sent the blindfolded recruit frantically patting around the table surface searching for the part. The instructor might even hide a small part in hs hand to observe the recruit's response when he could not locate it. The DIs watched the tests carefully and joined in the instructors' games. Later, we were told that those games had been played not to cause us to stumble but to simulate the ease of losing a part in the dark under combat. They stressed that a combat Marine must remember *exactly* where he puts each part during disassembly in order to reconstruct his weapon without the benefit of sight. And to think I didn't believe him when the colonel had said, "We'll do the thinking for you!"

A similar test was given later on the .45 caliber automatic pistol. Both of the tests were administered under large oaks in the area and were set up on four or five tables, each about two feet deep and ten feet wide. Three lines of us were waiting at each table, so those who were tested later were able to benefit from watching the first group. Guess in which group I was lucky enough to be a participant!

Later that afternoon, we had our first introduction to the infamous Marine Corps combat dinner—the C-ration. As generations of military men know, this is nothing more than a meal composed of olive drab cans of individual portions, prepared perhaps as early as World War II. There are usually cans containing a meat, vegetable, fruit, bread, cigarettes and candy, all enclosed in a cardboard box. Meats and vegetables are prepared in several combinations, but I never found any of them tasty. All I liked was the fruit. But then I never was in dire hunger, either.

That evening, all four platoons in the series gathered to "roast" the Marine Corps, DIs, military life and the Island in individual platoon skits. Each platoon had about an hour to write and rehearse its mini-play. Fear of the monsters had subsided, at least during this temporary respite, and each platoon performed for the whole series which were seated in the weathered sets of bleachers. At the end of each skit of about five minutes, the laden bleachers would shake under the roars of laughter and applause. All twelve of the series DIs stood around in small groups and watched as several of the platoon's skits dealt with recruit-DI conflicts. The skits always portrayed the DI as the bad guy and the recruit as outsmarting him in some imaginary conflict.

The sun had dropped past the horizon by the time the skits started, and only the greys of twilight were left to illuminate the performances. Laughter and applause echoed through the oaks each time one of the "DIs" of the performance was bested by the recruits, and even in the falling darkness the smiles of a few of the real DIs were evident. They weren't smiles of contempt either, but more like the smiles of parents watching their children put on a backyard play. Smiles that told us we had earned the right to poke some fun at our "parents" for the night. Although we were apprehensive, our joy and laughter were genuine.

I recall that one of the other platoons had a four-man singing group that undoubtedly gave the best performance of the evening. I don't remember which platoon they represented and I don't know the names of the individual singers. They claimed authorship of the words and melody of the song they performed. The melody was slow-beat, reminding me of the mournful work songs of Southern plantation life. The melody and lyrics were blended together in close harmony which astounded us all in its quality. The words dealt with a recruit unable to leave or change circumstances on the Island. It dealt with our real, day-to-day struggles, and each recruit in the bleachers could relate to the words drifting on the warm night breeze. The melody was unforgettable. One of the singers was a tall, black recruit with a deep bass voice, and I still can hear the echo of his voice as he reached the low notes.

I'm stuck . . . stuck here on Parris Island,
I'm stuck . . . stuck here on Parris Island,
'Cause I want to be a leatherneck . . . someday.
PT . . . I think it's gonna kill me,
PT . . . I think it's gonna kill me,
But I want to be a leatherneck . . . someday.

The last verse went like this:

One day . . . I'll leave Parris Island,
One day . . . I'll leave Parris Island,
And I'll be a leatherneck . . . that day.

I don't remember the other two or three verses they sang, but I do recall the feeling they produced that night. They sang about *us. We* were that song. When it was over, there was total silence for a short while, and more than one pair of moist eyes in the bleachers. We had all paid the price to sit in those bleachers under the oaks on that strange beach that night—together, yet alone. When each group of players was presented to the audience for judging, the singers won easily. They sang the song once more before we left to return to our platoon area. Strange, I heard the song only twice, almost twenty years ago, yet I remember it as though I heard it this morning.

We reached the 340 area and Egge gathered us around to explain plans for the night. We were to have fifty percent alert, supposedly to guard against "attack" by the unknown "enemy." All that meant to us was that one man in each tent had to be awake at all times, so Kidwell and I worked out our schedule. The rest of 340 did the same. The blackness of the night was complemented by the sleep-inducing sounds of crickets and frogs. But the sand fleas and mosquitos were persistent and sleep appeared to be impossible. I finally dozed off, leaving Kidwell on guard.

I was awakened by a commotion in the tent next to ours. I stuck my head outside in time to see the tent explode into the air. Ransom Downes was one of the occupants, but I don't remember who his partner was that night. The "explosion" was Rast, who after stripping off his utility shirt and "requisitioning" a recruit's chrome dome had slipped through the woods pretending to be an enemy penetrating our defenses. He had gained access to Downes' tent by whispering that the DI was coming and asking if he could get into the tent with the two men until it was safe to move about. Downes had started to move over to provide room for the "recruit" when Rast stood up, tearing the tent from its moorings. Rast then proceeded to chew Downes for allowing a stranger to talk his way into their tent. He pointed out that in combat both men would be dead. We watched in silence as Downes and his partner reassembled the parts of the tent and re-erected it in the dark. Later, we found that all three DIs were running around playing the same trick on various members of the platoon.

Sometime later in the night we were awakened by Egge, who told us of another game we were to play. First, he had awakened the black members of the platoon and told them to go hide in the woods, to act as though they had escaped from a P.O.W. camp. Then, the rest of us were awakened and told that we were to be guards, and were to recapture the prisoners and bring them back to prison.

We spread out in squad-size teams and filtered into the darkness, searching for the escaped "prisoners." Hours later, after stumbling through the blackness, we had captured all except Ronald Pender. Another group left in pursuit of the last "escapee." Although I wasn't on that squad, I later learned that it had found Pender but had to give chase through the woods to try and catch him. During the chase, Pender had run in and out of the edge of the tidal swamps along that perimeter of the Island. His capture had come about only when he tried to jump a small creek in the swamp. He didn't quite clear the water and fell forward in the soft mud, throwing his arms out in front of his body to break his fall. His right hand was deeply slashed on the razor-sharp edges of oyster shells in the mud. Bleeding furiously, he quickly gave up to his pursuers and returned to base camp to seek help and advice from the DIs. Egge and Rast soon arrested the bleeding and one of them took the frightened and bleeding recruit to the hospital. After Pender left, 340 finally retired for the night—what there was left of it. We didn't see Pender again until we returned to the squad bay the next afternoon, when we discovered that many stitches were required to sew up his cuts from the game in the woods.

The next morning, a Wednesday, we went through more equipment tests and evaluations before preparing for the return march to the barn. The march was long and tiring, and the DIs reverted quickly into growling, screaming monsters on the return trip. By the time we reached the Third Battalion area, we had been pushed and harassed back into pawns of the DIs. Elliott's Beach had been another deviation, however brief, from the fears and stresses of our training. A week from that day we would leave the Island. Less than a week left!

The next week would be a busy one for 340. The schedule would be almost nonstop. The tasks ahead looked like this:

Wednesday—Return from Elliott's Beach
Thursday, a.m.—Combat Readiness Test
Thursday, p.m.—Battalion Commander's Inspection
Friday, a.m.—Final Written Exam
Friday, p.m.—Final Drill Competition
Saturday, a.m.—Final Strength Test
Saturday, p.m.—Obstacle Course Competition
Monday—Regimental Commander's Inspection
Tuesday—GRADUATION
Wednesday—Greyhound and Good-bye!

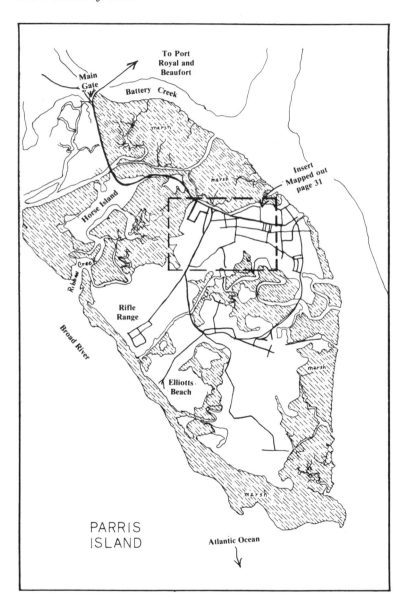

Main Gate

To Port
Royal and
Beaufort

Battery Creek

marsh

marsh

Insert
Mapped out
page 31

Horse Island

Ribbon Creek

Rifle
Range

Broad River

Elliotts
Beach

marsh

marsh

PARRIS
ISLAND

Atlantic Ocean

XIV

DRILL COMPETITION

XIV

O NE SYMBOL OF EXCELLENCE on the Island is sought by every DI and every platoon: a combat boot trophy awarded to the platoon which outperforms the others in close-order drill. The competition was held on the grinder at the Third Battalion, between our barn and Company Headquarters. I don't remember which officers and senior noncommissioned officers judged the competition, but there appeared to be about eight men on the judging platform that day.

Egge, Rast and Thomson had us out on the grinder practicing, pushing and sweating as we rehearsed for a week prior to the competition. We knew Egge wanted that boot for 340. Time after time, he had told us how important close-order drill was to him. The DIs pushed us even after dark in their review of each maneuver, each step and the manual of arms. We performed those drills in our sleep. Our boots were polished and rifles clean and shiny each day as we practiced.

Even Thomson had taken a hard-line approach to our trials, being more critical as we marched and practiced. He seemed to have more drive and determination during that last week. We were allowed no luxuries while the fate of the boot was at stake. The hot morning and afternoon sun bore down on 340 as we strived to please the monsters. Correct rifle position. Head and eyes straight to the front. Forty inches back to chest. Forty inches shoulder to shoulder. Swing arms six inches to the front and three to the rear. Again. Do it over. Don't bounce. March from the hips down. Over and over, then do it again. Egge. Rast. Thomson. The sun. Sweat. Chrome domes. When you halt, do it together, two counts. Snap. Look sharp. Strut. Over. Do it again. Practice. Think.

The results of all the training and practice looked good to us, but the monsters were never satisfied. Egge'e temper had become a short-fused stick of dynamite. Explosions were quick and painful. Rast, with Thomson, had joined in the pursuit of the boot, so all three had to be pleased. The margin of error was ever-narrowing, and the level of our skill was rising. The forced feeding by Egge was paying dividends, even if it was a liquid diet of our sweat.

We had practiced so much for this one competition that Egge had us to the point where he didn't need to call cadence. We did it with the sound of our boots hitting the grinder, and we were proud of it. We worked hard day after day, striving for praise from one of the DIs but ever sure there would be none. The many hours of working on the more complicated drill maneuvers helped us in the basics, since we had to count for ourselves in the special maneuvers. That silent counting forced each recruit to think about not only what he was doing but how his part related to what the rest of the platoon did.

On the morning of the final drill competition, Egge prepared us again by going over what we would do, one step at a time. In order to make our manual of arms maneuvers sound crisp and snappy, Egge had a tip to give us an edge. In our rifle cleaning gear was a steel rifle bore cleaning rod that unscrewed into four sections. Egge had us remove one of the sections of the rod, lift the hinged butt plate on the rifle and place the rod section up into a hole drilled into the rifle stock. (The opening is drilled by the rifle manufacturer and will store cleaning gear or an extra cartridge or two.) With that metal rod riding in the stock of the rifle, it would bang against the metal butt plate and emit a clear "clank" each time we changed rifle positions. It made the maneuver sound as though we were making the noise by slapping our rifles harder than our competitors were, which would be looked upon, we hoped, with pleasure by the judges. We practiced it several times and it did achieve the desired sound.

We would not wear chrome domes for drill "comp," as it is called in the Corps. Instead, we wore the soft cotton twill billed cap with the Marine Corps emblem stenciled on the front in bold black ink. When we were a new platoon, our caps had looked shabby, but while on the rifle range we had begun to starch them to make them look sharp and crisp. Each night we would place one of our two caps over coffee cans that the DIs obtained from the mess hall and give them a heavy coating of spray starch. Those "covers," as we called the caps, would stand rigidly for later use. For final drill comp, those covers would transform us into a platoon of crisp, snappy Marines, if only in our own eyes.

As the hour to perform before the judges drew near, nervous stomachs turned up, too. Even in their best DI demeanor, Egge, Rast and Thomson couldn't hide their nervous apprehension. Their repeated checks of our gear, even though they had thoroughly checked it that morning, showed their anxiety. Each DI had his own ideas about what we would have to do to win. Even the stoical Rast had some positive pointers to offer.

As we started our final preparation, each man was instructed to double-check his rifle and gear, then check the gear of the man in front of him to look for incorrect alignment of equipment and improper rifle position. We were told to whisper to the man in front if he needed to pull in his elbow or push it out to straighten the rifle. Egge sent us outside the squad bay with only one comment, "Let's go get the boot!"

Our reply was simple, "Aye, aye, Sir!" And out we went.

The day was hot, as usual, and we were confident, though nervous. Egge marched us out to the fringe of the grinder, where we stopped and waited for further instructions. Egge advised us that we were to be last in the competition, so he had us stand at the position of parade rest, that is, feet spread about shoulder width with the left hand behind the back and the right hand holding the rifle in place beside the right foot. We watched as the first platoon moved into position to get the competition under way. Egge cautioned us to watch our competition closely since we could take advantage of observing how the judges performed their task.

As the first platoon went through the required maneuvers, we were careful to watch each judge as he walked around the grinder, clipboard in hand, inspecting and rating the platoon as it went through its performance. Those judges missed nothing! Each time I felt I had seen something that didn't look quite right, I'd notice the judges writing on their clipboards. Each platoon had to perform a standard marching pattern which required it to execute essentially all the maneuvers of close-order drill. The routine, though standard, is extremely difficult. It is designed to test skills thoroughly, and it accomplishes that goal.

Our competitors were good that day. We knew after watching them march in front of us that it would be difficult to win this one. As each platoon finished, it would be marched to the edge of the grinder and positioned so the recruits could watch the remaining competition.

Suddenly, it was our turn. Egge turned to face us and slowly walked the entire length of the platoon. "Remember," he said, "look sharp. Think about what you're doing and what's coming next. Look crisp. Lean back. Let's go!" He called us to attention, marched us onto the grinder and halted us for a short pause, the signal to the judges that we were about to begin. Butterflies in our stomachs fluttered in their struggle for freedom. Two of the judges were already standing close at hand, clipboards ready, watching for 340 to do anything that would dock points from our final score. Egge, ready to present us for the judging, saluted the officer in charge, while Rast and Thomson watched from the sidelines.

He turned to us, and in his best leather-lunged DI voice, started the performance. As we stepped out in review, we put everything to work that those long, hot practice sessions had taught. Precision. Snap. Crispness. With each completed maneuver, our confidence swelled. We proceeded through the column movements, each man pivoting on the precise point of the man in front. Egge no longer needed to count cadence as our boot heels hitting the grinder set our pace to the beat. On into the flanking maneuvers next, our rifles gleaming in the sun, all in the proper position and all aligned to perfection. Each recruit concentrated on the task at hand and the results were obvious: it was 340's hour. We passed the reviewing stand of the remaining officers with all the precision and skill we could muster. The metal cleaning rod sections concealed in the stocks of our rifles enhanced each movement during the manual of arms segment, both while we were in motion and while we were stationary. Egge's advice was constantly on our minds. Rows of corn. Lean back. Strut. Don't bounce. A hundred thoughts raced through our minds to be checked and verified with each step—thoughts which had become second nature from all the rehearsal.

Then, almost as though time had ceased to exist, it was over. Egge had called the familiar command, "Platoon . . . Halt!" and we were waiting for the decision of the judges. The nervousness of performing was past, replaced by the nervousness of waiting as the judges gathered to total the scores of the competitors. We had returned to our position along the fringe of the grinder, where Egge quietly talked to Rast and Thomson. Rast was nodding his head, obviously in agreement with whatever thoughts were being whispered by Egge. Thomson walked slowly back and forth, hands folded behind his back. Each of us was dripping with sweat, as much from the nervous tension of the decision hanging in the balance as from the marching earlier.

I don't recall which of the judges picked up the bullhorn and made the announcement, but his words were clear, "The winner of the Drill Comp is . . . Platoon 340!" In one of the few such times while we were on the Island, an unchecked roar went up from our ranks. In short order, Egge marched us back on the grinder and halted us before the reviewing officers. His pride over the performance of his herd was obvious as the combat boot trophy was presented to him. I can still see him turning around to face us while holding that trophy, a broad grin directed at us. Without a word, and totally under the jubilance of the occasion, he winked! We were fairly intoxicated in the joy of winning. And Egge had winked at us!

Egge turned again to face the presenting officer. After another salute, the officer commanded to Egge that 340 had, in fact, put on one of the best performances he had seen and asked Egge if he would have 340 perform again for all those present to enjoy, not judge. For another ten minutes we marched in victory, bathed in the joy of fulfillment. We even performed one of the advanced drill team maneuvers we had practiced on those earlier summer evenings on the grinder. We stepped out in full confidence now, knowing that the sweat and earlier despair of close-order drill were things of the past.

We left the grinder under the admiring stares of our competitors and returned to the squad bay. Jubilant, we screamed with joy as we filed into the barn. The thrill of victory made us all light-headed. Even the DIs were caught up in our enthusiasm. Egge placed the boot on the DI's table at the head of the squad bay and called out, "Smokers, get outside!" That was a command we had heard only rarely since we arrived on the Island, and the eight or nine smokers, myself included, immediately reached into our footlockers for cigarettes and hurried outside with a resounding, "Aye, aye, Sir!"

The rules for smoking had the typical Marine Corps touch. We had to stand in a circle around the bucket one of the smokers brought out. Ashes and butts were to be placed in the bucket and disposed of properly once we returned to the squad bay. Each of us lit a cigarette, daring to talk to one another in the process. In the past, one of the DIs had remained with the smokers, but not this time. We were alone around the bucket, puffing and talking about our recent victory.

After the cigarette, we expected the DI to call us back inside. After a short wait and no sign of the DI, I lit a second cigarette, an unheard of luxury in those times on the Island. Two cigarettes. The other smokers also lit their second smokes. Still no DI. Another cigarette, then the fourth. Finally, the door to the squad bay opened and there stood Egge, hands on his hips, looking down on the group of smokers on the sidewalk. He called out to one of the squad leaders facing him in the group, "Cahill, how many cigarettes have you smoked?"

Quick glances passed among our little group around the bucket. Sensing Egge's light-hearted mood, Cahill replied, "One, Sir!"

As quickly and as genuinely as he had on the grinder earlier when he received the boot, Egge smiled, gave us the finger, turned on his heels and returned to the squad bay. We shared unparalled joy another fifteen or twenty minutes, smoking and talking before Egge called out for us to join the rest of the platoon. We found that while we were outside smoking, the others of 340 had the unheard of privilege of writing letters, right in the middle of the afternoon!

It was an afternoon of contradictions for a recruit in training at the Island. We had never before seen restraints lifted like that. As it turned out, we would not witness such a relaxed atmosphere again until graduation day.

XV

OBSTACLE AND CONFIDENCE COURSES

XV

ONE OF OUR TWICE-WEEKLY tasks was the running of the obstacle course. Envisioning that phase of our routine is simple if you can picture the following: an area about ten yards wide by fifty yards long strewn with manmade structures built of large timbers, round and square, which we had to climb over, balance on, swing under or vault over. I had an athletic background, so the coordination required was not difficult for me. Some of the others, however, did not have the upper body strength to maneuver themselves up and over the top members of some of the obstacles, a few of which had steel pipes as crossbars.

The first obstacle had a single steel crossbar about seven feet above the ground. The task here was to jump up and grab a steel bar about two inches in diameter, then swing our bodies up, grabbing the bar with our legs and rotating over the top. We simply dropped to the ground on the other side. A maze of other obstacles followed. There was a solid wall, about seven feet high, which we climbed. Actually, there was not much climbing since it had no footholds. It demanded that the recruit pull his body weight up with his arms, swing a leg up over the top, and drop to the ground on the other side. An overweight recruit or one who did not have adequate upper body strength struggled on these two obstacles particularly.

Each obstacle was separated by a distance varying from about two feet to twenty feet. Each demanded that the recruit do various athletic maneuvers for a specific distance and each required a specific muscular coordination. One obstacle required the recruit to pull himself up to a horizontal wood pole about eight inches in diameter. The pole was about five feet above the ground and resembled the temporary barriers one sees across highways where construction is taking place. After the recruit stood up on the round wooden cross member, he had to walk down another round wooden pole of the same diameter that ran perpendicular to the cross member. He had to balance himself as he walked the beam, much as one would when crossing a creek or a fallen tree. That pole, about fifteen feet long, was not on a level plane but sloped downward at about a fifteen- or twenty-degree angle. As the recruit finished the simulated "creek crossing," he jumped to the ground and continued to the next obstacle.

One obstacle required recruits, using the hands, simply to vault a series of barriers spaced about thirty-six inches apart. The barriers were a little over waist high, and good timing was required to clear one then continue vaulting over the next. Four or five of these were located about three-quarters of the way through the course. By the time we completed this phase, the tired muscles would start to rebel.

Several more obstacles testing coordination and strength led to the final challenge, the rope climb. The ropes were suspended from a square held in place at the corners by fifteen-foot telephone poles. Three or four ropes dangled from each side of the square. The entire course was wide enough to accommodate four or five men abreast at the narrowest obstacle. Two men started running the course simultaneously, side by side. Those waiting formed two lines behind the starting pair. As soon as the recruit in front had completed the first obstacle, the next would begin the course. It was not uncommon for the faster, more agile members to pass the slower recruits, so it was possible to have six or eight recruits ending at the rope climb at the same time.

I had been up and down rope climbs enough to consider them fairly easy. I was not aware that Marine Corps ropes were different from the ones I had climbed at the army camp in Columbia. The army ropes had knots in them about every twenty-four inches, allowing a good grip and a place on which to put the feet to push upward. Not so on the Island. Those ropes were about an inch and a half in diameter and hung from an eyebolt through the cross pole at the top, and there were no knots. It took effort and practice to learn how to climb that rope, touch the pole above the eyebolt, yell out our platoon number, then return to the ground.

At times we would complete the obstacle course, run back to the beginning and start the entire process again. Under the steamy heat of the summer sun, there were times when it seemed like a torture course that drained our energy and sapped every ounce of strength. I remember how Thomson and Rast would push us relentlessly, screaming and yelling to make us move faster. As our hands became slippery with sweat, making the last few obstacles became more difficult than ever. One recruit, McNally, was tall and had slender arms, making it extremely difficult for him to pull himself up over the bar on the first obstacle. I have vivid memories of his hanging by his hands from the horizontal bar, trying unsuccessfully to swing his legs up to it. While he hung there to catch his breath for another attempt, Thomson and Rast were looking up and screaming for him to hurry up, and running around him as he tried over and over to swing up to the bar. Eventually he learned to master the technique and the monsters were less demonstrative.

We ran the obstacle course regularly, though not daily, and with each completed run we became more proficient. We always came away dirty and sweaty, the sweat making the dirt adhere like glue. There came a day later in our training when all the practice and trials would be put to the test in a series competition.

While the obstacle course could be physically trying, it held no real fears for the typical recruit. That emotion was to be faced on the confidence course. While the barriers on the obstacle course rarely rose above six or seven feet, except for the rope climb, those on the confidence course rarely came below fifteen. That course was located another three or four hundred yards behind the mess hall and could not be seen from any of the roads.

Simply stated, the confidence course is a series of towers, ropes, cables and logs designed to conquer the recruit's fear of heights, and to bolster his confidence in his ability to scale hinderances he may encounter in combat. Once a recruit mastered this course, the intended result would certainly have been achieved.

This maze of towers reached heights of thirty feet on some structures and utilized varying methods both to scale and descend. The least difficult of these obstacles is the rope swing, a single rope hanging from a cross member directly over water. The recruits would have to approach the water (a moat about eight feet across) at a run, jump out and grab the rope and swing to the other side of the moat.

Some of the larger towers had more complicated twists. One of those was a large tower which looked exactly like a broad ladder made of logs. It was about twenty-five feet tall and the logs were six or eight inches in diameter. The difference between this ladder and one you normally use is that it was about eight feet wide, and as you climbed towards the top, logs were spaced wider apart than the lower ones. By the time the uppermost rung was reached, that space had opened to almost five feet. Once the top was reached, the recruit had to swing over the final rung and descend the opposite side. While cables helped hold the huge ladder-like structure in place, they were not tight enough to keep it from swaying with the weight of the recruits ascending and descending.

I remember standing on the second rung from the top and beginning to fling myself up to go over the top when the tower swayed. The motion caused my leg to miss the top and I fell back, hanging onto the top rung with all my strength until I found the next lower rung with my feet. My heart was in my throat that instant when my feet missed the rung. My hands were already slippery from sweat and I could picture my body flying through the air to the ground. I stood on the next to the last rung a second or two, took another deep breath and attempted again to swing to the top. That time, the tower didn't sway and I made the crossing safely and descended the other side. As I reached the ground, Egge walked casually by, his hands behind his back. Without looking at me, he asked sarcastically, "Having fun, Miss Moore?" I screamed, "Yes, Sir!" and ran to the rear of the line for the next obstacle.

Another obstacle was a tall A-frame type structure built on a platform about fifteen feet above ground. The top of the A-frame was another ten or twelve feet higher, resting against a round log cross member which was bolted to two telephone pole uprights. Ropes dangled from the cross member to the ground. Each recruit had to climb a shorter rope at the other end of the platform, walk the length of the platform (which had open spaces between eight-inch diameter logs which served as a floor), climb the A-frame and descend the ropes. Not too difficult if you had no fear of heights and followed the instructor's directions.

If you did have fear of heights, it was tested on one of the final obstacles of the confidence course. The structure didn't look complicated, simply a raised platform about thirty-five feet in the air and about fourteen feet square. Three sides of the raised platform had handrails but the fourth side had no barrier. Two cables, an inch and a half in diameter and about six feet apart, were attached to a pole on the back side of the platform at one end. The ropes sloped down over the open side of the platform and continued in a sharp decline over a manmade body of water about thirty yards across. The cables were anchored to a post about six feet tall along the far side of the water. From the side, it had the general appearance of a rope attached to the roof of a three-story building, with the other end attached to the top of a ground floor door of a building across the street, only the street was replaced by water.

By now, you've probably guessed that each recruit had to climb up the platform and descend by way of the cable stretched across the water. That much is correct. But in the descent, each recruit had to cross the water the Marine Corps way. The first one-third of the distance was covered by balancing on top of that cable, carefully drooping a leg over one side of the cable and locking the other ankle over it, and slowly inching down the incline, balancing the remainder of the body weight on the cable by positioning it directly under the stomach and chest. We were face down as we eased away from the platform, with nothing but a narrow cable to keep us from falling into the water thirty-five feet below.

After the stomach crawl for the first one-third, we had to stop, swing our body under the cable and bring our legs up, locking our feet together over the cable. Our weight would be supported by our hands and ankles as we hung from the underside of the cable, facing the sky. We descended this second third by easing one hand over the other down the cable, using our ankles as guides.

The final one-third was the easiest. We simply turned loose with our ankles and, suspended by our hands, finished the chore hand over hand until we reached our destination. That final segment was not only the easiest physically, the distance from the ground gradually decreased.

The DIs liked to play games on this obstacle. A DI would watch from below until a recruit reached about the halfway point on the cable descent, then yell out, "Miss _____, what's the correct position of attention?" When the recruit had recited the official description, the DI would yell back, "Well, Sweetheart, . . . snap to it!" The recruit would then attempt to snap to attention and fall feet first into the water to the amusement of the instructors.

I do not have a fear of heights, so the altitude did not cause any hesitancy on my part. However, I did see sheer terror on the faces of several platoon members who scaled this obstacle, and what I saw was no pretense. For them it was a harrowing experience. Their knuckles whitened as they put a death grip on the cable, and they shook with fear as they eased out over the edge of the starting platform. There was no way to avoid descending the cable. The monsters saw to that. Sadistically, the DIs seemed to delight in making paratroopers of the recruits who feared it most. Since the water under the cable was only four or five feet deep, a falling recruit could wade ashore, but for those who feared heights, knowing that the water below was shallow gave little consolation. The DIs would force enough recruits to fall that none of us knew if he might be next. The only possible redeeming value I could see if a recruit fell was that he received temporary relief from the broiling sun.

We went over the confidence course only a few times. The DIs, especially Egge, would harass and push each man to increase his speed, stressing the need for swiftness in combat. "You move that slow in combat and you'll be dead!" he would scream out. "Hurry up!" His voice echoed through the huge Spanish moss-covered oaks, ever pushing, relentless.

XVI

FINAL
FIELD

XVI

HE DAY BEFORE WE GRADUATED, Monday, was an important day for us: Regimental Commander's Inspection, also known as Final Field Inspection. The DIs told us we had to pass or we could be set back in training. The threat of being set back. particularly at this stage, would serve to encourage each of us to do his best.

Basically, the inspection was carried out by the Regimental Commander and his staff to determine if each recruit in the series had absorbed the principles set forth in his training. The physical inspection included examination of our rifle and inspection of our uniform and overall appearance. Since our first day on the Island, each of us had been preparing for this event. It was stressed to us that qualification badges had to be in *exactly* a specified position on the uniform. The belt buckle had a correct alignment. There was a proper procedure for tucking the shirt into the trousers. Each crease in the shirt had to be positioned to a precise standard. The inspecting officer would go over each item of clothing thoroughly, as though the turning of the very earth depended upon it. He would then do the same to the recruit's rifle. "If you're going to be a Marine," Egge had told us, "you'd damn well better look the part."

We knew that the inspecting officer would be looking for any small infraction, anything to show a lack of attention to detail. We had shaved earlier that morning for the inspection, but even with a close shave, fine hairs escape the sharp blades. These soft hairs or peach fuzz are almost impossible to remove. In typical fashion, Egge had discovered a way to remove them. It was easy. Simply singe them off! Before you form a picture of sixty-five recruits giving one another third-degree burns with lighted matches, I'll say now that it did not burn at all. The flame was passed over the hairs rapidly and lightly, and they promptly disappeared! No pain and no trace of the fuzz at all! Simple yet effective. Only then did we discard the matches, assured that our shaves would pass the test.

Looking the part was only one phase of the inspection. What made Final Field so intimidating was that the officer and staff inspecting the recruit would also question him. Questions could cover any phase of training experienced, including classes and practical application. As I think back, I suspect that many of the fears were simply that we may have forgotten some small fact and felt certain we would be questioned about that very fact. We had been faced with an avalanche of new information since we arrived in June. Certainly every detail could not be retained. Yet, no one could afford to answer a question incorrectly with such potentially disastrous consequences hinging on the response.

We spent hours going over everything from the chain of command to our General Orders, and including the obvious history and firearms courses taught in the classroom. Each of us studied his notes hungrily as he stood outside the mess hall after meals. I no longer had interest in my stick-figure art or daydreaming, only in passing Final Field. I was confident, but still didn't want to leave anything to chance.

As a platoon, 340 was also preparing for Final Field. The DIs, all three of them, wanted one hundred percent to pass the inspection. The day before the inspection was spent cleaning, polishing and preparing each item of the uniform and rifle. Loose threads, called "Russian ropes," had to be clipped from the stitching of shirts and trousers. Shoes had to have the regulation spit shine and brass buckles had to sparkle. Each recruit inspected his own gear, then sought the nodding approval of the DI.

Then came the rifles. We cleaned and inspected, inspected and cleaned. Then we'd do it again. Egge, Rast and Thomson could inspect a rifle with the best of them, so we could be sure that if we passed our DI's inspection there would be no problem with Final Field, at least on that phase. Individual parts of the dismantled rifle were scrubbed, cleaned and inspected. The rifle was closely inspected again after reassembly.

The storage room in the squad bay was small, perhaps ten feet by twelve feet, and we stored our rifles here overnight instead of leaving them hanging in the customary position on our racks. One of the DIs brought a vacuum cleaner from home and placed the operating appliance on the floor in the storage room to suck lint out of the air to keep it from settling on our rifles. We placed clean white towels on the shelves of the storage room and made the room as dust free as possible. The final cleaning of the rifle, after all the preliminary inspections by the DIs, was done wearing gloves. I don't know where the DIs acquired all the gloves; we were only concerned about what to do with them. After the final cleaning, the DI, also wearing gloves, would approve the completed task, and then we placed the rifles in our hospital-clean room for the night.

After the rifles were stored, the DIs reviewed us on our classroom notes. They would make up questions, point out a recruit and have him answer. That cram session lasted all evening, with each recruit striving to retain as many hints and clues as possible for the coming inspection. Egge also had us recite the words to "The Marines Hymn" that night.

The next morning we counted off, went for our morning run, had breakfast and cleaned the squad bay. Then came the final preparations for Final Field. Meticulously, each of us dressed in his "tropicals," the khaki summer dress uniform, and again went through the final checks of his appearance and that of his bunk mate.

After we retrieved our rifles from the "sanitized" room, Egge advised us that there was one change in our plans for Final Field. We would go out for inspection *without* Pender, the recruit who had seriously cut his hand at Elliott's Beach. Egge explained that Pender could not pass Final Field since his hand would not allow him to execute properly the required handling of his rifle for the inspection. Therefore, Pender would take all his personal equipment and be locked in the storage closet!

We were shocked that Egge would permit anyone to miss a required inspection, and yet many of us, myself included, envied Pender a little. We would be outside in the heat undergoing our sternest inspection, hoping and praying we would pass, and Pender would be sitting inside doing nothing. Obviously the records would show that he not only participated but passed!

When the time arrived for us to fall outside, Pender was locked in the storage room with instructions not to answer any inquiries from outside or utter a sound until one of our DIs opened the door. Egge then walked down the center aisle and ordered, "340 . . . On the road!" This time Egge instructed us to walk outside, not to run, since he didn't want anyone to mess up his shined shoes or rumple the tightly tucked-in shirt.

We were marched over to the grinder across the street behind the mess hall, where we waited at parade rest for the inspecting officers to appear. By now, the butterflies in my stomach had started to flutter, and I mentally went over as much training information as I could in those final few tense moments. The sun was hot, but the small beads of sweat forming on my forehead were caused by stress since I had become accustomed to the intense heat. A photographer was taking candid photos of us and I was aware of his presence to my left as he snapped frame after frame for publication in our platoon book, which we would receive after we left the Island.

Finally, the officers appeared and the inspection was underway. When one of the officers stepped in front of me, I smartly snapped the M-14 to the position of inspection arms. In that position, the rifle is held close to the chest, diagonally, with the bolt open and ready for inspection. The officer addressed me in a conversation that I still recall. He took my rifle, and as he checked it for rust and dirt, he asked, "What's your service number, Private?"

I answered with as much authority as I could muster, "Sir, my service number is 1865693!"

"What's the serial number of your weapon?" he then asked.

Again, trying to sound confident but not cocky, I responded, "Sir, the serial number of my rifle is 210044!" As I answered, he held the rifle so that he could check the accuracy of my answer, then quickly demanded, "What's your fifth General Order?"

I knew that one, too, and answered, "Sir, my fifth General Order is to quit my post only when properly relieved!"

He handed the rifle back to me and looked over my uniform from my cover to my shoes. During this visual inspection, he asked, "What's your seventh General Order?"

"Sir, my seventh General Order is to talk to no one except in the line of duty!" I replied. He hesitated a second, then as he turned to go to the next recruit, all he said was "Good!" That had to mean I had passed the last obstacle. Final Field was over. I was elated!

After the entire series had completed the inspection, we returned to the squad bay and found that we all had passed. Even Pender, who had to be released from the storage room! We were a happy lot, and those buses were beginning to get closer.

Two more days and we'd leave here! Forty-eight hours! 340 had a funeral to attend, its own—and we would not miss it for anything in the world. Not now.

XVII

GRADUATION

XVII

T UESDAY, SEPTEMBER 10, 1963. The big day. The end in sight. To say we started that day like all the previous days would be an understatement. How could this one possibly be like the others? I don't remember which DI had spent the night, but he had no trouble waking 340 that Tuesday. Most of us could have awakened the DI.

We went through our morning count-off and for the short run before breakfast. I felt as though I could run until graduation at 10:00 a.m. if the DI wanted. As we entered the mess hall with its aroma of coffee and bacon, I realized that I would eat only one more breakfast after this one in Third Battalion. I wasted no time in finishing my meal and walked outside to fall in platoon formation, standing at attention. This day there were no notes to hold in front of my face, and I simply waited.

We returned to the barn, ready to prepare for the ceremony. Egge, Rast and Thomson could sense how we felt. They had brought us this far, and the final touches of graduation and out-posting were only frosting on the cake. We would graduate in our tropicals, the same dress uniform we had worn for Final Field. Our rifles and 782 gear had already been turned in to supply. Since we had passed all our tests, we were simply waiting for the parade to formalize our "certificate of completion" of the recruit training phase of our Marine Corps experience.

The day was clear and sunny with only patches of thick white clouds high in the sky. An early fall breeze was blowing in from the harbor that morning, but summer refused to give in to the cool weather of fall and the day would be another hot one. That didn't bother us; if it had been a hundred and fifty degrees or snowing, it wouldn't have dampened our spirits. Not this day. We had a date with a band. They had a song to play. For 340. Us!

We finished cleaning the squad bay and dressed to go over to the parade ground by the statue of the flag raising on Iwo Jima. Each recruit checked his own uniform repeatedly, then inspected the uniform of his bunk mate. Shirts were tightly pulled and tucked into trousers. Imaginary flecks of dust were softly brushed off shoes. Rifle badges were positioned on shirts an eighth of an inch above the left breast pocket. Hats were cocked low over the forehead, giving the finishing touch to Corps standards. Egge, Rast and Thomson passed up and down the center aisle, inspecting and giving a helping hand or suggestion where it was needed. No screaming and yelling now. Their herd was ready. Egge gave the long-awaited order, "340 . . . On the road!"

We answered in unison, "Aye, aye, Sir!" There was no need for Egge to have us repeat that one. They probably heard it in downtown Beaufort.

We joined with the other three platoons in our series for the half-mile march to the parade grounds.

All the officers of our company and series were there for that last march, plus the company and series sergeants. The Company Commander was Capt. Golden and our Series Commander was Lt. Curtis. Sgt. Lampka was the Company Sergeant, and the Series Sergeant was Sgt. Pearman. Each platoon proudly displayed its senior flag at the head of the platoon. We presented a fine picture as we marched the short distance, proudly stepping out under the cadence of the DIs.

After we crossed the road and reached the vast grinder, the whole series was halted and we stood at parade rest, waiting for the time to begin the ceremony. We were less than a hundred yards from the reviewing stand and bleachers, and a crowd had already formed, sitting in the stands and looking out over the soon-to-be-graduated recruits. Somewhere in the throng were my mother, Kathy, future mother-in-law and future sister-in-law, Sharon. I never could make out their faces in the crowd, but I knew they were there. We were not in front of the stands, rather about fifty yards out. The Parris Island Marine Corps Band was in full dress, entertaining the crowd with martial music until time for us to march in review.

We were an anxious group of recruits, even though we wouldn't be recruits much longer. We had been through all the caverns of hell that I ever wanted to explore . . . and then some. I kept telling myself we had earned the right to be here; but there were thoughts of recruits such as Miller who had arrived with us yet remained somewhere in another platoon. Reflecting came easy now that the hard part was over. The heat of the summer had felt almost unbearable at times. There had been times of frustration, humiliation and even desperation. Rifles, chrome domes and cartridge belts all covered with sweat and dirt. Finished. The steady pop of distant rifle fire on the range. Snapping in. Over. The nights of lying in bed reciting the words of "The Marines Hymn." Gone. It was almost our song.

Egge, Rast and Thomson stood in front of 340, waiting to present us for graduation. Rast towered over Egge, and I looked at them waiting rigidly for the command to start the parade. Thomson had walked to one side of the platoon and was just returning to his position as I stole a glance towards the crowd.

The wind was strong enough to hold 340's flag out straight, rippling the fringe. I looked at the huge American flag on the Iwo Jima memorial. The monument was behind the stands, alongside the road, and the huge flag was gently swaying in the breeze. The stands by now were full, and the officers had taken their places in the reviewing stand. My stomach churned in anticipation and there was a dryness in my throat. I remember wanting a sip of water right then. Just enough to wet my tongue and throat.

The band had stopped playing. The time had finally come. An officer in front of the reviewing officers gave the command, "Pass in review." Egge turned towards us and called the platoon to attention. We popped our heels together and stood waiting for the command to proceed. At Egge's bull-horn voice command, we started. It was here. At last! We were marching step by step towards the completion of twelve weeks of training. The band was playing a military march, and we kept in step by hitting our left heel on the grinder with each beat of the bass drum. To some of the career veterans present that day, we may not have looked like seasoned Marines, but *we* felt like we were. Lean back. Strut. Strut. Strut. We were proud. Rows of corn.

We marched for the reviewing officers and for the crowd in the stands, and were halted at a position facing those gathered for the ceremony. We stood rigidly at attention for all to see as one of the Island's ranking officers gave a short speech to the graduating troops. Then, in a short ceremony, the top five recruits of each platoon received their PFC stripes. Suprisingly, time seemed to pass quickly as we stood in the mid-morning sun.

I remember the officer's finishing his short speech by expressing his wishes for our continued good luck in the future and saying "Congratulations!" We were then called to attention and stood in pride as we awaited the next command. Then it happened, catching us by surprise. We knew that it would happen today, but we hadn't known just when. The band started to play. The notes were crisp and the melody was a familiar and glorious one. They were playing *our* song! *"The Marines Hymn!"* At long last, it had become *our* song, and it had an emotional impact on us all. From somewhere inside, I had the feeling of freedom for the first time since I came to the Island. There was a knot in my throat that I couldn't hold back, and I felt warm tears rolling down my cheek. They were tears of relief, as though someone had lifted a great burden from my shoulders. I felt a little embarrassment until out of the corners of my eyes I saw tears shed by my fellow recruits. Each of us had faced the trauma of Parris Island, and a release of emotion was being expressed by each of us as the band played. That song signaled the end of our daily stress and torment. The tadpoles of 340 had come full cycle. Our transition was complete. In the short time it took the band to play that song, the pressure had been relieved. The tears had been the faucet that flushed our emotions. We were graduates. They played . . . our song.

I remember an officer's directing the order to all the DIs, "Sergeants . . . Dismiss your platoons!" They were actually going to do it! As soon as Egge tells us . . . it's going to be over! We hung for a lifetime, waiting as each DI turned to face his herd and pass on the command.

Egge faced us, hesitated a fraction of a second, then bellowed, "340 . . . Dismissed!" We had only to acknowledge his command, which we literally screamed out, "Aye, aye, Sir!" took one step back, and it was over. Each platoon in the series went through the same process.

As the last platoon completed the acknowledgement of the command, a roar erupted from the entire series. Hats were thrown into the air. Recruits hugged one another. We were in ecstasy. I remember shaking hands with Kidwell, who was next to me. Then I saw Downes, my partner in the oleandor caper, and we shook hands and patted each other on the back.

I noticed that spectators from the stands were walking towards us. The silent tears were quickly brushed aside as our joy erupted again. Then I saw Kathy and started running to her.

We met in a strong embrace and the celebration was genuine. Everywhere on that grinder were joyous friends and family, hugging and sharing in each new graduate's happiness. Small groups gathered close around the beaming new Marines. Those whose friends and family were too far away to make the trip were drawn into the other groups. At that moment we in 340 were as close as we had ever been. Yet, at that same moment, the separation of the individuals in that family was beginning. We were now to start another phase of training away from the Island. We would no longer face the world as one.

We left the grinder after the graduation ceremony and showed our friends and families where we had lived, trained and sweated for the last three months. I stood for pictures with Kathy and family beside the Iwo Jima monument, as did most of the other recruits. Each time a platoon member came by, we called out to him, introducing him to our guests. Laughter, which had become a rare expression of our emotions, at last erupted from deep inside, its sincerity solidly felt.

We crossed the street for a short walk to a building where there was a counter and tables, similar to a canteen. Inside was air conditioning and freshly cleaned and waxed vinyl floors. My guests and I found a table and sat down. We ordered Cokes, coffee and, as I recall, some danish rolls. As I looked around the room, I recognized other faces sharing smiles and experiences with their guests. While we were enjoying the long-awaited opportunity to be together, I was surprised to see a handful of our series DIs enter the room. Things seemed to quiet down as they entered, but they joined in our celebration, congratulating recruits—make that graduates—as they passed through the room.

As Egge approached our table, I jumped to attention automatically. I remember Egge's telling me to sit down and relax. That was no easy command to obey, but I did. I introduced him to my guests and he stayed a politely short time, then moved on to talk with other graduates and their families.

Pop music blared from a speaker on the wall. The atmosphere was alive with our jubilance.

I spent the remainder of the afternoon with my loved ones. We drove to most of the places on the Island where I had trained at one time or another during boot camp. I pointed out specific places either important to the base or significant in my own personal struggle with the training. The range we qualified on. The barracks we stayed in while at the rifle range. The obstacle course. The confidence course. Elliott's Beach. They all seemed less menacing now. Had 340 tamed them? Or did they tame 340? They looked serene now. I had a sense of accomplishment that was comforting to me. I never expressed that feeling to my guests, but they all knew and loved me enough to sense that feeling. I pointed out the different platoon flags we passed. We saw only one senior platoon carrying the flag with the fringe, and I knew the recruits' feelings as we watched them pass, marching with their stiff backs and the steady beat of their boots on the pavement. Damn, I felt good that day!

The afternoon passed quickly. I had to be back in the barn about five o'clock, so we drove back to Third Battalion. We arrived at the small horseshoe-shaped drive in front of the barracks and saw other graduates saying good-byes to their guests. We, too, stood in the shadows of the moss-draped oaks and said good-bye. I would not see my family and loved ones for another month since we would be taken to North Carolina to go through Individual Combat Training for a month before receiving leave. This good-bye was easier than before since the Island stay was over—almost. At least I could rest easy about that. I watched them drive away, waving as they pulled out into the street and passed back by the front of the barracks. Our last full day on the Island was drawing to a close.

When we went to chow that evening, we ate in a relaxed mood for the first time since we arrived. Instead of waiting in platoon formation to return to the barn, we simply straggled back in groups of two or more. I ate with Bill Rich that night, and I remember we were both still on a high from the day's activities. We had paused outside the mess hall and watched a platoon going through close-order drill on the grinder. It was not a new platoon, but it had not yet reached "senior" status either. Its DI had just completed his instructions on a maneuver and we watched as he took the recruits through practice.

I looked at Rich and commented, "They look pretty good." We had only graduated that morning, but now we could critique as though we were seasoned veterans!

We watched in silence a moment longer before Rich spoke, "Not as good as 340!" We looked at each other, laughed and turned to walk into the barn.

As we stepped into the squad bay, I sensed a different feeling in the air. I couldn't quite put my finger on it at first, but it was there. As I started to pack my seabag for the all-important bus ride in the morning, I was struck with the realization that there was no tension! And we were talking to one another! Out loud, not in whispers. We moved around the squad bay at will. Never had we had such liberty. Egge, Rast and Thomson were still there, but they were casually sitting and talking among themselves—and to some of us! It was so tranquil it was almost frightening. Or would have been if we had not been so happy.

After we finished packing our seabags and showered, Egge sat us down for a talk. He talked *with* us, not *at* us that night. We asked questions about what we would do at Camp Lejeune, our next stop. Questions about the options of duty stations and schools. Questions about specialized training. And many more. Egge, Rast and Thomson answered all of them to the best of their knowledge and ability. They displayed patience and understanding, traits we had no previous indication they possessed. Egge told us what we could expect in our next month's combat training, and assured us we would never be treated like recruits again. That caught our interest! He advised that since we had completed training on the Island and had graduated, we would never again be touched physically by our instructors. It was finished. That part of our Marine Corps infancy was complete and would never resurface. No more fear. No more fists. No more abuse. I'm sure he answered an unasked question in all our minds, and we rested easy from that moment on.

We prepared for lights out after Egge talked a while longer, and we lay in our racks in the dark after Egge flipped the switch and took a last walk down the center aisle. His heels echoed in the darkness with each step. Each of us was in his own dream world of thought while listening to Egge's steps, waiting for him to disappear into the DI's house. The soft light from the shower room cast enough light to silhouette him as he slowly paced down the aisle. His features weren't distinguishable in the dim light, but I knew every line and crease in that face. The Smokey-the-Bear hat was cocked, as usual, low over his forehead, and the shadow he cast on the floor was a long, narrow black reflection of the man. He stopped for a second about three bunks before reaching mine. Outside, the crickets chirped and squeaked. From some other barracks on the Island came the voices of another platoon, distant yet clearly audible as they responded in unison to a command of their DI, "Aye, aye, Sir!" The sounds of taps had already died out. Egge stood, feet spread, hands on his hips, and in a low, normal tone spoke, "340 . . . *Sing* me *our* song!"

We didn't acknowledge his order with the customary "Aye, aye, Sir," but simply started singing. By the fifth or sixth word, we were singing in unison. Not the loud, boisterous version that one could expect, but a rendition as reverent, as moving, as personal, as an anthem of a private fraternal organization. As we sang, Egge walked back down the squad bay, turned at the far end and slowly walked back up the aisle. He reached the entrance to the DI's house and turned around to face the platoon as we finished the last verse. As the final words of the song drifted into the night, there followed a short, poignant pause before Egge uttered three words it took us twelve weeks to earn: "Good night, *Marines!*"

XVIII

PARRIS ISLAND GOOD-BYE

XVIII

ALONG WITH SEPTEMBER 11 came the anticipation of departure. We had packed our seabags the night before, and no counting off was ordered that morning. Rast and Thomson were both there for reveille, along with Egge, who had spent the last night with his new Marines. For the first and only time while we were on the Island, Egge did not flick the squad bay lights off and on to wake us up; he simply switched on the lights and called out, "Good morning, Marines!" I had heard the other DIs arrive and was lying awake in my rack waiting when the lights flipped on, as were most of 340. Our systems had long since become accustomed to waking up at the same hour each day. We responded to Egge's greeting with a hearty "Good morning, Sir!"

We went about the usual morning rituals of preparing for the day . . . the final day! After dressing, we began to fall outside to go to the mess hall for breakfast. As we approached the door, a strange rumbling noise was apparent outside, a noise which I first heard about the time I got up. We exited the barracks as we had done so many times during those three months to find our dreams-come-true.

In the early mist of dawn were five of the most beautiful, shiny Greyhound buses I've ever seen! They were parked at the curb in front of our barn, idling, just waiting to take us away. The drivers were standing together in a group talking as the early morning sky revealed streaks of grey. The interior lights of the buses were on, allowing a view of row upon row of plush seats, like velvety thrones upon which to whisk us quietly away from the grasps of the Island monsters.

Graduation was over. We had passed the tests. The band had finally played our song. We floated over to the mess hall under the all-familiar sound of Egge's cadence. We snapped smartly through the chow line, a little salty now and proud. As I sat down at the table with my back towards the window, I heard a DI yelling and screaming outside. Without bothering to look around, I could tell that a young platoon was about to enter for breakfast.

As they moved down the line, trying to side-step for their DI, my assumptions were confirmed. The recruits had freshly shaved heads and cowered expressions familiar to all Marines. When they had finished passing through the chow line, they gathered around one of the tables. One of the new recruits read grace from the plastic-coated card, and the DI bellowed, "Ready . . . Seats!" As with us earlier, the DI had them do it another three or four times before he let them eat. One of the scared young recruits facing my table looked my way and our eyes met. He had the uncertain look of a frightened puppy, and I remember smiling at him. He quickly dropped his head, looking down at his tray full of food, pretending he hadn't seen the smile. I had hoped the smile would be interpreted as a smile of "Good Luck," but then I realized he probably thought I was on permanent duty there and was in some way testing him. I had finished eating and was drinking the last drops of coffee when their DI screamed at a recruit for looking around. It wasn't the recruit I had smiled at, but he was at his table. The DI had done a magnificent job of giving in to the monster. I thought back over the last three months and shuddered. I felt sad for that recruit, but joy at my own knowledge. As I reached the exit door, another recruit platoon was entering through the front door. I turned around as their DI roared at them, "Do it again, Shithead!" I turned my back on the scene and stepped out into the gathering light.

We returned to the squad bay to make final preparations for our departure. Before breakfast, we had stripped the sheets, blankets and pillow cases from the bunks, folded them and turned them in at the supply room. Next we had folded over the mattresses on each bunk and placed the now-empty locker boxes on the bare springs half of the lower bunk. Our only remaining possessions were our packed seabags, also on the bunks. As I sat on the edge of my bunk, I thought back to the night before when Egge had sat us all down around the DI's table for our last evening together.

Egge praised our performance during training and expressed his pride in 340's accomplishments in the various platoon competitions. We grew silent, though, when he turned to the subject of discipline. "You may not agree with what I'm going to tell you, but I want you to know, either way." He paused here, looking over the whole platoon. We had no idea what was coming, but we could tell he was serious. "The reason you were disciplined the way you were wasn't because I enjoyed it. I did it because you may, God forbid, find yourself in combat. When and if that time comes, you will have to be ready. In combat, it's your life or your enemy's, and that's the final judgment. If you're in a foxhole in the night, and some Gook jumps in that foxhole while you're firing in another direction, the first thing he'll probably do is either shoot you or hit you with his rifle. If he shoots you, it's over. But if he hits you, you've got a small fraction of a second to react, and what you do in that split second may determine whether you live or die. The shock of being hit is something you have to experience to be prepared. If you have not been hit, then you will probably not react fast enough, and you may die. Well, you have been hit, and you know the pain, and you know how to accept that pain and react instantly.

"Your chances of surviving are better for that. Now if 340 is in combat, and only one of you survives because of that ability to accept pain and still continue, then all I've done has been worth it."

As I sat, the shock of his words still echoing in my ears, I looked around the squad bay. We had turned in our rifles and 782 gear on Monday after our last inspection, and the bunks looked strangely bare without the packs and rifles hanging on the end where they had faced the center aisle for so long. 210044 was now as much a part of my past as was my innocence. Already, the squad bay exuded a feeling of nostalgia. No more would 340 shake the walls in acknowledgement of commands to fall out for drill, P.T., classes, meals or obstacle courses. No more sweat on the concrete floor from "watching TV." No more "moving house." No more field days. No more monsters. The buses had finally come. 340 was ready.

Egge's command "340 . . . Outside!" brought me back to the present. Another hearty "Aye, aye, Sir!" was echoed back by all of us, joyously. We were going through the doors for the last time. The concrete floor felt harder and the steel bunks looked cold and vacant as I stopped at the door for a final look back. The seabag was slung over my shoulder in the fashion it was the day I first entered the squad bay. The DI's table and chair sat vacant now, a silent sentinel awaiting a new herd. In that brief look back, endless thoughts crossed my mind. Egge's ever-present commands—"340 . . . On the road!" "Chrome domes, cartridge belts and rifles, stand by to fall out for drill!" "Again!" "Well, Ladies, you'd best snap outta it and get with the program!" "Outstanding, Private, out-fucking-standing!" All the memories would stay with me, and that squad bay was ready now to join my past. I turned and exited, knowing that even in my absence I would leave a part of me in the barn. I left my sweat, which no amount of cleaning will remove. I left my fears, after learning that only I could conquer them. I left on schedule, something I had doubts about earlier. But best of all . . . I left.

Outside, the buses were loaded quickly with our gear and we climbed aboard. I sat about halfway back on the righthand side. Egge, Rast and Thomson waited until we were seated, then boarded the bus. Thomson and Rast finally let their smiles show as they walked down the aisle speaking to their graduates and spreading wishes for good luck in each new Marine's direction. Egge followed, pausing at almost every recruit to speak some words of encouragement or cheer. When he reached my seat, he reached out to shake my hand. As we firmly grasped hands, I realized that I had never shaken hands with him before, and I probably never would again. His grasp was as firm as I had suspected it would be and he looked me straight in the eye as he spoke, "Moore, remember . . . one foot in front of the other. Good Luck!" I remember mumbling something like "Thank you, and good luck to you, Sir." He smiled and replied, "It's not 'Sir' anymore, just Sgt. Egge." From months of habit and repetition, I could only reply, "Yes, Sir!" He smiled understandingly and continued down the aisle.

In another few minutes, Egge, Rast and Thomson left the bus and stood on the sidewalk between the righthand side of the bus and the barn. Our excitement continued to build and we talked among ourselves. There was a short pause, as one of the buses in front of us was not quite ready. An eternity seemed to pass before the driver finally raced the engine, pulled the door closed and eased the bus in gear. As the buses in front of us started to move, we knew the end was near. Just get us through those gates!

I looked out the window back to my right to see Egge, Rast and Thomson still standing on the sidewalk. Some of us waved good-bye to the three of them. The bus driver had turned the air conditioning on and had left it on while the bus was idling waiting for us, and it was refreshing to feel the cool air as I waved to the DIs. Rast and Thomson raised their hands in a final good-bye. Egge did not. We were his herd. 340 had grown from an infant to maturity, and he had been a part of that growth. We had sweated for him. We had performed for him. 340 was completing its final day's existence. A wave is too casual to express the passing of something that is a part of you. If I outlive all my children and my children's children, I'll carry the vivid image of my last sighting of Egge standing there on that September morning. Just as the bus began to move, he snapped to attention, offering us his farewell in a way that only Egge would have thought of. The sight was indelible. Egge in the morning sun, appropriately in front of the barn—saluting us!

As the buses turned on the road to head for the gates to the Island, the realization of our goal of leaving that place was infectious. Laughter rang out, for the first time in months for some. We were on the way! We broke out in the most appropriate of the old rifle range songs, but now with new words:

No more days left for us, Honey, Honey
No more days left for us, Babe, Babe
No more days left for us
Now we're on that Greyhound bus,
Honey, oh Babe, be mine.

The driver had a task to do, but he watched our gaiety in his mirror. The two-mile ride to the entrance was cool, but anything but quiet. As the bus crossed the bridge, though, an odd silence came over the passengers slowly. The gates were now in view through the front windshield, and we leaned out into the aisle to look. By the time the bus reached the gates, there was absolute quiet. Eagerly, we watched the buses in front of us pass through. Deep down inside, something told us that Parris Island would not be over until we passed through those gates. Forget that the band played our song. Forget that all our gear was loaded.

Forget that we had our travel orders. Forget that the DIs had been left behind at Third Battalion. Get through the gate! Until we did that, anything could happen. This was the last obstacle. And it was in view.

As the tail lights of each of the four buses in front of us slowly slipped past the sentry, we could hear the roar of the new Marines even though the windows of our buses were closed. The sentry stood on the left side of our bus and waved us through, too. Our bus driver even today may have hearing problems as a result of the uproar and pandemonium as we saw the sentry a final time through the rear window. The roar when the buses left the barracks was like a whisper compared to that as we passed through the gate.

It was finally—and irreversibly—over.

EPILOGUE

I HAVE COMPLETED MY ACCOUNT of the events which occurred to Platoon 340 while I was in Marine Corps boot camp. Even now, after all the years, there are times when I recapture the emotions we experienced during that basic training. A white-hot August afternoon sun beating down has reminded me often of the fears and stresses of a sweat-soaked recruit trying to please a demanding DI, a recruit filled with the knowledge that his inept efforts could result in physical punishment from that same DI.

Memories of that training are as clear to me now as they were when each incident occurred. That doesn't really surprise me.

What does surprise me is that I have formed some opinions which may be in direct conflict with the opinions I had while I was going through that experience. I can't account for what other people believe and don't advocate that their opinions should rest on my experiences. I know what the harsh training did to 340 and I can't accept the position of Marine Corps hierarchy that the abusive techniques we encountered are "incidents" outside their guidelines.

What I do believe is that the time has arrived for the Corps to stop playing games. I think their training tactics and techniques should be a matter of public record, adhered to by both the Marine Corps and training cadre. I believe the public, for the most part, could accept recruit training incorporating corporal punishment if that system applied only to volunteer trainees. Most of the Corps' problems have come about because its "official" position has always been "we don't believe in" that kind of training. Technically, that may be true. In practice, it's a different story altogether.

In what may appear to be a contradictory position, I will state for the first time publicly that I support the disciplinary techniques the Marine Corps handed out to 340. Before you label me a pervert or misfit for supporting corporal punishment, continue reading. Don't lump me with warmongers and sadistic psychopaths. Hear me out before you hang me out.

I happen to believe also that no war is just. That no war is fair. *No war,* period, is what I would prefer. But I'm enough of a realist to conclude there will never be a time when war will not exist somewhere on this earth. I abhor the atrocities and tragedies of war, both physical and mental, and yet I cannot eradicate them. Not the wars. Not the atrocities. Not the tragedies. That leaves me only one alternative. In the event of war involving me and my country, I must be trained in survival tactics, assuming there can be survivors in a modern war.

I want to be prepared as best I can for what I must face. I want to be apprised of the realities that I can expect to encounter. Two of the realities faced by all combatants in a war are fear and stress. Even though I may be expert at firing the weapon at hand, if I cannot deal with these two abstract realities, there is a very real possibility that I will not return from battle.

You may think Marine Corps training is too harsh and too brutal, especially after reading the account I've presented. Well, the Marines put about fifty thousand men a year through Parris Island, plus thousands more through San Diego, California. Those men will assure you that the Corps will take you to your limit in stress, and probably scare the hell out of you in the process. I've been there and I know that fear. Fear cannot be explained; it must be felt. Those DIs on Parris Island introduced me to that fear and showed me I could deal with it. They could not have accomplished that task without some form of corporal punishment. What other effective means, or vehicle, do they have to teach fear? Surely one cannot teach fear in an atmosphere of tranquility. Can fear be taught through a movie? Through classroom lectures? If those are your suggestions for teaching a man how to deal with fear, you've never experienced the real thing—terrifying fear.

What about stress? Can it be any less prevalent than fear to a man who must fight in a war? Shouldn't he be taught how to deal with the unrelenting stress he is going to face? Can he cope with watching his comrades in arms being blown into oblivion or maimed for life? What about that kind of stress? What about the stress of simply now knowing whether you will live another day? Classroom, you say?

Since the basic concept of the military is to perform strategic combat functions, men must be sent to war prepared with the best training and knowledge and armed with the best equipment available. To do any less is an injustice to the soldier. I don't have all the answers. In fact, since I have never fought in a war, there will be those who say I'm in no position to offer suggestions. Their opinions are no less valid than mine and their right to express those opinions is no different from mine.

Corporal punishment was not looked on by most of 340 as a pivotal point of training. It was simply a fact of our day-to-day training life. We accepted that part of our training the same as we accepted the heat or the summer rain. Each recruit had to perform his best as an individual or he had to pay the penalty. As a group, 340 had to stand together according to the dictates of the DIs or suffer the consequences. The corporal punishment and abuses were only tools to prepare us for a potential combat role.

I use the words "abusive" and "corporal punishment" knowing full well that they are accurate when applied to 340. The choke hold of Rast was physical abuse. When he, Egge and Thomson hit recruits with their fists—or even dealt open-hand slaps—it was corporal punishment. Maltreatment of recruits existed when Willard was forced to drink Wisk and water until he threw up. It existed when Downes had to eat the Tabasco sauce-covered cookies. Throughout this narrative, I've described some of those incidents to expose what we had to deal with daily. I could not describe each and every violent act I saw or felt since those incidents took place every day.

I know that the official Marine Corps position is that the DIs do not resort to physical abuse or beating of recruits, and that if such acts do occur, they are isolated incidents and do not reflect the norm of basic training. Don't try and sell that to 340! We lived under the unofficial discipline rules—twenty-four hours a day. We lived in fear of the monsters, a real and justified fear for our health and safety. We knew that if one recruit screwed up, the whole platoon could expect to be punished in some manner. I knew about the reputation of Parris Island before I signed up for the Marines. I've talked to hundreds of other Marines since I left boot camp, and they have confirmed that they were subjected to the same abuses and maltreatment we experienced. Abuses such as my beating for having guests, and Willard's and Downes' punishment, were identical to experiences of other

Marines on the Island at other times. So when the Marine Corps hierarchy suggests that these are just "isolated incidents," they are either covering up, lying or blind. Let's strip away the dark clouds over training tactics and techniques. Let's have training to deal with all phases of combat readiness, including fear and stress. Let the Marine Corps use their "340 discipline," but let them be straight forward about it. Tell the men before they leave for Parris Island what they're going to see and experience. Don't keep it hushed up, then spring it on them behind closed doors after the fact. Make it totally voluntary; that's the only way to involve those new men in the system.

Let the Marine Corps build men the same way they've been doing unofficially for generations. Their record speaks for itself. They know how to teach men what to do to be effective in war. They have a proud tradition of producing elite combatants, ready when needed to be "first to fight." Let them use the training techniques and tactics, honed by generations of DIs, that have proven effective. Don't sell them short on their ability to produce results.

If a war comes and I'm physically able, then you need not ask if I'll go, because I will. I believe each of us owes this country more than his tax dollars. I'm willing to carry my responsibilities to the combat zones, if necessary, to protect the interests and future of my children. One of the reasons I feel that way is my background in the Marine Corps. I've had my discharge papers for a number of years, but I'm still a Marine. A part of me still lives under the watchful eyes of the Eagle, Globe and Anchor. I still get a tightening sensation in my chest and a lump in my throat each time I hear "The Marines Hymn." I'm not ashamed of that. It brings back memories of that summer in 1963 when a group of us faced the traumatic training system of the Corps and succeeded in achieving the skills necessary to become Marines. It brings back memories of the Millers and the Angiones, the Richs and the Downes, the Palmers and the

Houchins, and Willards and the Penders and of our trials during that training process. Each Marine Corps recruit platoon has its individuals who become welded together with a pride and spirit which intensify until it becomes as much a state of mind as it is a state of being. Yes, the Marines did strip away all my individual rights during those three summer months of recruit training on Parris Island. Yet, out of that deprivation came a firmly rooted appreciation for those very rights and privileges, and a desire to ensure their durability.

A Marine Corps advertising slogan, no longer in use, explains exactly how I feel about their training, "Nobody wants to fight, but somebody better know how."

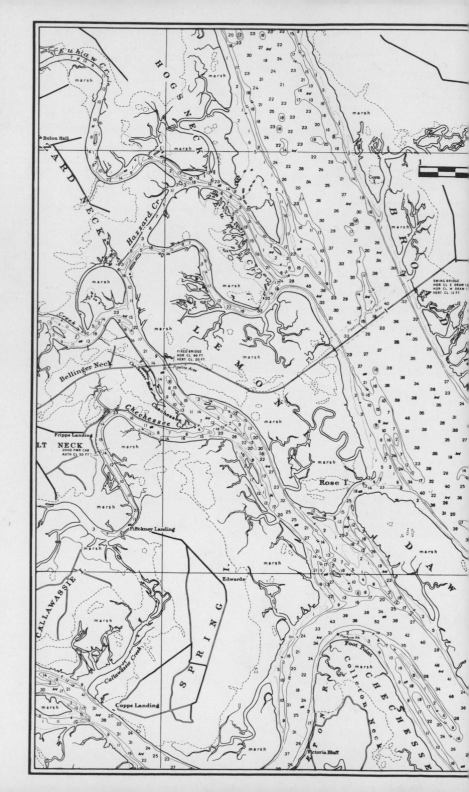